Organize,
Communicate,
Empower!

**CORWIN
PRESS**

The Corwin Press logo—a raven striding across an open book—represents the union of courage and learning. Corwin Press is committed to improving education for all learners by publishing books and other professional development resources for those serving the field of K-12 education. By providing practical, hands-on materials, Corwin Press continues to carry out the promise of its motto: **"Helping Educators Do Their Work Better."**

Organize, Communicate, Empower!

How Principals Can Make Time for Leadership

HEIDI SHAVER

CORWIN PRESS
A Sage Publications Company
Thousand Oaks, California

For information:

Corwin Press
A Sage Publications Company
2455 Teller Road
Thousand Oaks, California 91320
www.corwinpress.com

Sage Publications Ltd
1 Oliver's Yard
55 City Road
London EC1Y 1SP
United Kingdom

Sage Publications India Pvt. Ltd.
B-42, Panchsheel Enclave
Post Box 4109
New Delhi 110 017 India

Printed in the United States of America

Library of Congress Cataloging-in-Publication data

Shaver, Heidi.
Organize, communicate, empower! : how principals can make
time for leadership/by Heidi Shaver.
    p. cm.
Includes bibliographical references.
ISBN 0-7619-3141-4 (Cloth)—ISBN 0-7619-3142-2 (Paper)
   1. School principals—Time management. 2. School management and
organization. 3. Educational leadership. I. Title.
LB2831.958.S43 2004
640'.43'0243712012—dc22

                                        2003018445

This book is printed on acid-free paper.

Acquisitions Editor:	Robert D. Clouse
Editorial Assistant:	Jingle Vea
Production Editor:	Kristen Gibson
Typesetter:	C&M Digitals (P) Ltd.
Cover Designer:	Michael Dubowe

Contents

Preface

Being offered that first leadership position is initially invigorating. You start to think about all you hope to accomplish and the powerful impact you will be able to make on the lives of children. You are bubbling with enthusiasm, and you can't wait to get started. You wait with anticipation for school to begin and then the day finally arrives. Teachers file in followed by children; your time no longer appears to be your own; district personnel begin to slide you policy and procedure manuals along with a plethora of managerial duties laden with deadlines; parents begin to call and question building activities; the roof begins to leak; the custodian decides to take an unapproved leave; supplies ordered in the spring are lost in the warehouse; last year's administrator overspent the budget, and you are notified that your current budget is being slashed to compensate for this overspending; and on, and on, and on it goes! And we wonder why new leaders burn out so quickly and rush back to the classroom or out of education all together.

What about experienced leaders returning for their fifth, seventh, or fifteenth year as an administrator? They have had some time off to rejuvenate, are familiar with the routine of school procedures, their office staff are experienced and efficient, and so they approach the beginning of the year with energy and a new sense of purpose. These experienced leaders walk into the building on their first day back and learn that the ground rules have changed just a bit. New policies have been adopted over the summer that have resulted in some additional job duties; assessments have been revised in order to better align with state standards; additional positions have been created at the district level, and individuals learn that they not only have a new supervisor, but that the means by which they will be evaluated has also changed; guidelines have been established to ensure greater consistency, which is a definite plus, yet experienced leaders know their staff well enough to realize that the gap between where the staff currently is and where they are expected to be is as wide as the Grand Canyon; three staff members have come in to voice their concerns about the new reporting procedures; parents call to demand a change in their child's room placement; two staff members have decided to accept positions at other sites; and on, and on, and on. And we wonder why so many of our experienced leaders begin to seek options for early retirement!

Of course, there are some deeply rewarding moments that leaders, both new and veteran, experience during the first few months of the school year, but leaders so often find themselves so overwhelmed that they can't find the time or the energy to savor them. So, how do leaders in today's world rise to the occasion and meet the demands placed upon them?

Organize, Communicate, Empower! How Principals Can Make Time for Leadership was written to address this very question. This text will provide leaders with strategies and techniques related to Organization, Communication, and Empowerment, three areas that I see as foundational to effective leadership. My goal is to equip leaders with tools to make the complex job of leadership manageable so that productivity can be increased and energy sustained.

About the Author

Heidi Shaver is a senior consultant with Cutting Edge Learning, Inc., a consulting group devoted to providing support and ongoing professional development for teachers, administrators, and educational leaders. As a senior consultant, Heidi works with school districts and instructional leaders to design and implement training opportunities to further develop literacy and/or leadership skills for educators. In addition, she offers individual and small group coaching related to work efficiency, data analysis, and designing and implementing long-range professional development plans. Finally, she also designs and facilitates staff retreats that foster increased collaboration, communication, and commitment among team members.

Prior to the development of Cutting Edge Learning, Heidi was an elementary school principal at Century Elementary School in Aurora, Colorado, and an assistant principal at Clyde Miller Elementary School in Aurora, Colorado. Before entering administration, Heidi spent 15 years working within the Aurora Public Schools as a classroom teacher, literacy support teacher, and administrative resource teacher. In addition to her full-time work in the public school arena, Heidi has also dedicated time over the course of the past eleven years to designing and delivering professional development opportunities for school districts across the country as both an independent consultant and a trainer with The Wright Group Publishing Company.

Heidi has her Colorado Type D licensure from the University of Phoenix and a master's degree in Elementary Reading from the University of Northern Colorado. In addition, she earned a bachelor's degree in Elementary Education and Special Education from the University of Northern Colorado.

Heidi is blessed with a wonderful husband and three beautiful daughters. As a family they enjoy exploring the zoo, mountain camping trips, and vacationing with family in the Great Lakes. Heidi also spends spare time writing. *Organize, Communicate, Empower! How Principals Can Make Time for Leadership* is her first published text.

Acknowledgments

There are a number of individuals to whom I am indebted for bringing the ideas and thoughts within this book to print. First, I would like to acknowledge and thank the wonderful leaders I have had the privilege to work with during my educational career. Judy Griswold, Dianne Dugan, John Dale, and Dea Kreisman not only helped to shape my beliefs and practices by serving as strong role models, but also allowed me to grow as they extended their trust and confidence in my abilities as a leader. I would also like to thank Susan Olezene for her continued support and wisdom over the course of the past several years. Susan's amazing ability to see the parts within the whole and connect information from various contexts kept me focused and grounded as I worked with my staff. In addition, I extend my gratitude to Rich Rusak, who served as my mentor, colleague, and friend. Rich provided me with insight, guidance, encouragement, and a sympathetic ear when times were tough. As the Director of Leadership Development he truly lived up to his job description, assisting me in identifying my goals and then stepping back to allow me the independence to forge my own path with my staff.

Last, I would like to extend my deepest gratitude to the staff of Century Elementary School in Aurora, Colorado, who took me under their wing, extended to me their trust, and allowed me to be a part of their family. They stood with me as I lead, forgave me for my mistakes, and served as a constant reminder of the true joy of teaching. Without these caring and dedicated individuals I would not have been able to realize my goals and potential as an educational leader. Gung ho, my friends!

Heidi Shaver

Corwin Press gratefully acknowledges the contributions of the following people:

Martin Hudacs
Principal
Avon Grove High School
West Grove, PA

Diana Casas
Principal
Terrell Wells Middle School
San Antonio, TX

Colleen Reeve
Principal
Collier Elementary School
San Antonio, TX

Mike Parnell
Principal
Carrollton High School
Carrollton, MO

Dedication

This book is lovingly dedicated to my husband, Dan, and my three beautiful girls, Maggie, Emily, and Julia. They have consistently been my source of strength. Their undying patience, love, and support were the staples that allowed me to put thought to pen.

Introduction

The traditional role of a school administrator or principal encompassed a variety of managerial tasks including, but not limited to, budgeting, scheduling, managing discipline, hiring and overseeing staff, ordering supplies and materials, and completing a wide range of district and, in some cases, state reports. In order to complete all these tasks efficiently and effectively it was necessary that building leaders develop sound skills and strategies specifically related to organization, time management, and communication. Programs designed to prepare individuals for leadership positions offered instruction in the development and use of these core skills, and leaders entered the profession with a sense of security in knowing that they were prepared and ready to handle their first leadership position. In addition, new leaders often served in apprenticeship types of roles as assistant principals or student deans where they were able to get their feet wet in the field and further refine and develop essential skills while under the care and support of an experienced master leader. This picture is not the reality of educational leadership today.

The shift into the Technology and Information Age, characteristic of today's society, led to numerous changes in the educational arena. Accessing and processing information has become far more relevant and necessary than the memorization of facts, higher-level thinking skills related to synthesizing information to make generalizations and draw applicable conclusions have become essential, and those entering our workforce today must be equipped to appreciate one another's talents and work collaboratively to keep up with the demands of an ever-changing and dynamic world. So the demands placed upon teachers have shifted, which has ultimately changed the role of the educational leader. Instructional leaders of the 21st century need to be adept at juggling an enormous amount of tasks far beyond what was traditionally expected.

Leaders today must be able to analyze and evaluate test data; design differentiated professional development to increase student achievement based on the observation and evaluation of personnel; effectively communicate with all types of personalities; and work collaboratively with staff, parents, and community members to determine students' needs and oversee the implementation of best practices rather than a specific program with a predetermined sequence of skills in addition to the managerial tasks associated with the traditional role. Also, with the decline in the number of individuals entering the profession of educational leadership, many first-time leaders will enter positions without the benefit of serving in an apprenticeship role. In other words, they must be prepared to hit the door running and manage a leadership position independently, without the direct support of a master leader.

What this means for leaders entering the profession today is a need for a wider spectrum of skills and strategies to handle the daily job requirements of an educational leader. The most obvious reaction to this change is to attempt to discard some of the more traditional tasks and replace them with more challenging duties such as analyzing test data and designing professional development programs to assist staff members in meeting students' needs, but this simply is not feasible, considering that the traditional duties of a building principal are still a piece of the larger puzzle. Unfortunately, leadership development and licensure programs have shifted their focus toward these more challenging, dynamic issues, leaving a void regarding the managerial tasks previously taught.

With such a multifaceted role, and sometimes less-than-adequate preparation, new educational leaders must begin to look deeply at the core of what is required of them in order to discern the foundational skills that, if fostered and developed, will allow them the time to take on the greater challenges. The purpose of this book is to address this core and to provide new leaders with methods and strategies for efficiently taking care of the technical managerial tasks, in order to make time to develop into the instructional leaders that they aspire to become. In his book, *Beginning the Principalship*, John Daresh (2001) identifies technical skills, socialization, and self-awareness as three broad areas supported by research as being key to leadership effectiveness. He also notes that when those new to the profession or in the process of completing licensure programs were asked to rank order those three areas, technical skills were viewed as the most critical to success. It is important to recognize that all three of these areas are critical, but surviving the first year often depends on a leader's ability to juggle the technical aspects of the job efficiently in order to allow for more time to work on the other areas. This text highlights techniques, strategies, and skills related to *Organization, Communication,* and *Empowerment.* These three areas are the focus because each offers opportunities for a leader to increase productivity and make the most out of each hour of the day. Development of skills within these three areas is essential if one is to perform effectively as an educational leader in a modern society where the demand to perform as an instructional leader, while continuing to take care of the millions of details of the job, is the reality.

> *"When you come to the edge of*
> *all the light you know, and are about to*
> *step off into the darkness of the unknown, faith is*
> *knowing one of two things will happen:*
> *There will be something solid to stand*
> *on or you will be taught how to fly."*

Barbara J. Winter

Section I

Organization

Some individuals are naturally organized. They possess the innate ability to take a disheveled closet, desk, or even room and with the touch of magic hands, transform it into a space where everything has a place based on its purpose and use and everything is in its place. These are the individuals who invented organizer units for closets, small cabinets with mini drawers for nuts and bolts found at hardware stores, and of course the modern refrigerator complete with labeled storage doors and compartments of all different shapes and sizes. For these individuals, organization is simply not an issue. Their brain compartmentalizes everything for them, they naturally see ways to make a hectic schedule flow and devise creative ways for juggling a wide spectrum of tasks on a daily basis. If you are one of these people, congratulations!!! You probably know a lot more about this topic than the rest of us, who simply have to muddle through and devise survival tactics to make our lives and jobs more organized. If you are with me and find yourself wishing you had innate organizational skills, then this chapter is written specifically with you in mind.

Some highly unorganized people might be wondering why all the hype about organization? They may feel that they have made it through so far, just fine, functioning in their natural, unorganized, cluttered manner. There is only one reason to consider developing skills in organization if you don't already possess them naturally, and that is that it will positively impact your productivity.

In the name of simplicity, this section has been organized—well maybe I do have a bit of that left brain mentality in me—into three chapters: Organization of the Facility, Organization of Time, and Organization of Programs. Each chapter provides useful, simple tips that can assist a leader in becoming more organized, which will lead to increased productivity. Basically, you will get more done in a shorter period of time, leaving you with more time to spend in the classrooms supporting teachers, a key necessity in becoming an effective educational leader.

Chapter 1

Organization of the Facility

Organizing the work environment is a critical piece to ensuring that work not only gets completed, but does so in a timely manner to meet deadlines. In addition, as projects are in process it is essential that they can be quickly located to make short work periods productive. Organization of the facility also pertains to the entire school environment. It is absolutely amazing how much time is lost when materials for staff meetings are spread haphazardly throughout a building and have to be collected or located each time a meeting is scheduled. Keeping a well-maintained and organized school environment also serves as a positive model for students and teaches them the effectiveness of order and organization. Various aspects related to the organization of the facility are described below under the headings of files, stackable shelves, meeting space, and hallways and community areas.

Files

The first step to getting organized with paperwork is determining the main categories to use within a filing system. It may be helpful to begin by developing a list of general topics that you feel will warrant a section for filing. As you develop the list, subheadings may become apparent, which will lead you to decide whether to use more generalized categories followed by subtopics or if you wish simply to alphabetize all topics. For example, "Scheduling" is a main category that leaders will need to establish a file for within their system. But to keep things truly organized for easy retrieval, this category will most likely be too broad, thus developing subheadings within this topic such as parent communication, afterschool clubs or other activities, assemblies, schoolwide performances, sporting events, and the like, may be helpful. Once you have identified the general categories to use within your filing system you can begin the process of organizing your workspace to allow for efficient filing.

Depending on the space in your personal office or workspace, files can be organized in a variety of ways. If you are limited in terms of space, you will find that simply keeping files in a cabinet or drawer within hanging files labeled in alphabetical order is the easiest solution to organizing information and projects. In addition to a basic cabinet in which files are arranged in alphabetical order, it is also important that you develop a location for a set of files that you work with often. Keeping these in an upright file stand on a desktop or counter makes them easily accessible. For me this meant my coaching file, book study folder, general monthly newsletter file, staff bulletin folder, and grade level or course expectations. This information was constantly being referred to and information was added to these folders quite often, so it made sense to keep them in a more accessible location rather than within the general filing cabinets.

If you have the luxury of several areas for files, then you can get a bit more creative with organization. You may wish to have a drawer or separate location in which you have working files for individual staff members, teams, work groups, or departments. Teacher, team, or department newsletters, special projects, grade level milestones and assessments, and team or department meeting minutes and agendas can all be organized within this area. These would be in a location separate from the official confidential personnel files that need to be kept in a locked location.

In our times of heightened accountability and assessment driven instruction, it might be useful to dedicate a filing drawer or cabinet to assessment. This could contain site and district assessment protocols, guidelines for administration of assessments, assessment schedules, parent letters and informational flyers, and of course data analysis sheets that include the analysis and evaluation of assessment results.

Finally, you will want to start a personal growth file for yourself. This file will be a central location for items that demonstrate your own growth as a professional leader. You may wish to include supportive letters from staff or parents, long-range professional development plans that you have designed with your leadership team or individually, flyers from conferences or seminars you participate in, and personal goals that you have established for yourself. Make sure to include a time line that defines activities you have planned to assist you in reaching your goals. This file will become a wonderful portfolio to share with your supervisor and/or mentor and will serve as a reference for them as they write your evaluation.

Whatever system you design for filing information within the workspace, it is critical that you clearly explain your organizational system to a secretary, office clerk, or other employee who will be designated to support you on a weekly basis with filing information. With that in mind, it may be helpful to label the outside of cabinets or drawers if you do decide to have a more complex system than simply organizing the files in alphabetical order. Of course you will also need to help filers by identifying the main topic area under which paperwork is to be filed. This aspect is addressed in the next section on stackable shelves.

Stackable Shelves

Stackable shelving units provide an effective means for organizing information in an office. Two shelves placed on the corner of the desk directly within the office can be used by a secretary and the leader to move information in and out of the office. The top shelf is for incoming mail  and information and the bottom unit is designated for outgoing information. Usually, more comes in than goes out on a daily basis, thus the reason for the top shelf, where more space is available, being reserved as the "in" location. Colored file folders can be used in conjunction with the stackable shelves as a visual notification of specific types of information or mail. For example a green file folder might be used for items requiring a signature, and a red folder might be used for information that needs immediate attention. As with anything, if you expect your secretary or office personnel to use the system efficiently and effectively, you will need to train them in how the system works. Ensuring that your office staff is clear on the type of information to go directly to the circular file, rather than into your in box, will keep "junk mail" reading down to a minimum.

A second set of stackable shelves can also be a valuable resource to the leader in managing and organizing information within the office. A set of four stackable shelves together located in close proximity to the leader's primary workspace, most often near a computer, can be labeled to organize information as follows:

Top Shelf:	Daily Projects
Second Shelf:	Long-Range Projects
Third Shelf:	Waiting for Response
Fourth Shelf:	Waiting to Be Filed

Daily Projects: This shelf should contain projects to be completed that day. For those individuals who are used to making lists, this location is for the Must Do activities for the day. Of course it would be wonderful to empty this tray each and every day, but this may be an unrealistic expectation. Things will come up that force a change of pace and an adjustment to plans. This is the reality of the job. A key piece to making this system work is to evaluate the projects to be done at the conclusion of each day. By reviewing incomplete tasks remaining in the *Daily Projects* tray, as well as upcoming priorities, you can make sound decisions regarding what needs to be placed in the *Daily Projects* shelf for the following day. This daily review takes only a few minutes (no more than 5) and will save precious time the following day when you will be organized to hit the door running. A large number of leaders will tell you that they waste the majority of their time first thing in the morning as they slowly move about their workspace determining exactly what they will focus on for the day.

Long-Range Projects: Throughout the year, leaders will face a number of long-range projects to complete either independently or in a collaborative manner with staff members. It is these types of projects that are organized in this second shelving unit. If a leader has more than one long-range project to work on at a time, the projects can easily be separated within this shelf using colored file folders. The actual organization of tasks for completing long-range projects will be discussed in Chapter 2 of this text.

Waiting for Response: Often leaders will complete a task or project only to be left waiting to get additional information or approval from a third party. This third shelf is a location designed to keep track of those projects or tasks. It can also serve as a reminder file for checking back with people who fail to respond to initial requests or proposals. By looking through this shelf on a weekly basis, leaders will keep on top of things that are currently out of their hands.

Waiting to Be Filed: This shelf will grow the fastest and can become quite unwieldy if left unattended for long periods of time. A number of the items that a leader touches will at some point end up filed. This shelf is designed to temporarily house those items until time is available for filing to occur. By attaching a small sticky note with a file label on the top of an item before placing it in this shelf, anyone who is familiar with the filing system can perform this timely task. If attacked weekly, the filing can usually be handled by another trained staff member in less than 15 minutes. This is a nice contrast to a leader personally spending five hours filing information at the end of a quarter. Keep in mind that some things simply don't need to be kept. In other words, the circular file may be the most appropriate location for an item that you will not need to refer to in the future.

Meeting Space

Regardless of where meetings generally take place, maintaining a set of essential materials for meetings in a central location will save you an enormous amount of time and energy. For those lucky enough to have a designated staff meeting room, keeping a stocked cabinet complete with critical consumable items is a simple way of ensuring that everything that might be needed is available and ready on the spur of the moment. Below is a listing of items that may be useful to keep stocked in the supply cabinet:

- Sticky notes of various sizes
- Wide colored markers
- Pens and pencils
- Writing tablets or notepads
- Sentence strips
- Masking tape, glue sticks
- Highlighters (set of 6 containing different colors)

- Extra overhead transparency sheets
- Staplers (2 should suffice) with a backup pack of staples
- Scissors (3"-5" adult size)
- Note cards
- Name tags (1 package for meetings with parent groups or community members)

In addition to the items mentioned above, it is also important that a meeting room location contain an overhead projector, computer, and LCD panel, where available, screen, flip chart, and pad of chart paper. If space in a building is limited and a separate room to use for meetings is not available, then keeping the consumable items listed above organized separately in a couple of plastic containers and housed in a specific location in the main office or in a supply closet will work just as well. Make sure to designate a materials collector within the group to routinely pick up these supplies and bring them to scheduled meetings and then return them to their designated location in the office at the end of each session. Leaders may also wish to designate a media or technology person to be in charge of making sure the necessary A-V equipment, computer, flip chart, and chart paper for recording make it to the meeting room ahead of schedule. By identifying A-V needs on a weekly events calendar, those designated to support the leader will know in advance what is needed, and as a leader you will always be prepared.

Having all the necessary supplies organized and ready in advance is a time-saving strategy that will allow you to spend precious time before a meeting planning and organizing content and processes to be used, rather than running about gathering necessary supplies.

Carefully planning processes and transitions, and establishing routines at the beginning of a meeting will also save time later on. Materials that are needed for a meeting should be placed out on tables beforehand so that individuals are not scrounging around for what they need to complete an assigned task during their precious work time. To assist you in clean up, designate a materials gatherer at each table to collect supplies and return them to the plastic containers or the cabinet in the room.

Considering and planning the room arrangement is another technique to saving precious time during an actual meeting. For example, if you wish to have staff members sit together in grade-level teams or by departments, place table tents ahead of time to designate where they should sit when they enter. This will save transition time later on after the meeting has begun. Likewise, if you are seeking open sharing of ideas and clear communication during the meeting, then hold the meeting in a location where chairs can be organized in a semicircle or horseshoe without tables that serve as barriers. Of course, this may not be feasible for large group meetings where 70 or 80 staff members will be in attendance. If you are truly after interaction and want all staff members to be able to contribute to discussions equally, you will need to form smaller discussion groups and designate an individual within each group to serve as a recorder and facilitator. Prior to the meeting, facilitators will need to be provided with training and direction regarding the processes for managing the discussions and materials that they will need to gather. Recorders will need to be prepared to share their groups' information with the larger group after discussions are completed, or written records can be posted for others to review.

Finally, think through strategies for grouping or regrouping participants during a meeting ahead of time to make transitions occur quickly and efficiently. Below are a few suggestions for placing participants into groups:

Colored candies: Groups are formed by the type of candy each selects, or groups must contain one of each type of candy.

Playing cards: Distribute cards to all members, then have them suit up (e.g., diamonds, spades, etc.), or have them form groups where all suits are represented.

Birth month: Have participants line up by birth month and then form groups of a specific number starting at either end of the line.

Colored dots: Place colored dots on handouts and have members group themselves according to their dot color. (This technique works well if you want to arrange groups ahead of time to ensure diversity among members.)

Numbered dots: Place a number inside a colored dot on handouts and have members first group according to their dot color and then switch to form different groups by numbers. (Make sure to have table tents prepared to identify where groups are to meet so participants don't waste time wandering around looking for group members.)

A note of caution to the zealous new administrator who walks into his or her first administrative position and begins the first formal staff meeting by asking all 110 staff members to group themselves according to the type of candy they selected upon entering the auditorium or commons area: We all act and respond based on purpose. If we understand and have been given a meaningful purpose behind a new experience, we will more than likely be willing to give it a try. But without this knowledge, rarely will we leap into the unknown blind. So, the 110 staff members who have just been told to group themselves by candy type may react in any or all of the following ways:

- Happily follow the directions because they enjoy change and diversity, laugh, and simply sit back down,
- Ignore the direction and form their own groups based on pre-established cliques within the building,
- Openly complain about having to do something so ridiculous, or
- Comply only to save their personal venting for the staff lounge later that afternoon.

Unfortunately, the number of individuals who react in the positive manner as described by the first bullet will be in the minority. So, you may wish to begin your first full staff meeting outdoors or in a gym where you can engage them in some nonthreatening and fun game-type simulations to drive home your message of building a cooperative and collaborative staff that works together, remains flexible, and is open to new ideas. Any number of the activities described in team building books such as *201 Icebreakers: Group Mixers, Warm-Ups, Energizers and Playful Activities,* by E. West, can be used to meet this purpose (see the Resources for a list of these types of books). Another option might be to talk with a building physical education instructor or one of the school coaches for ideas that they use with students. One activity that I have used successfully in the past to get at the key concepts discussed above is Moon Ball. The procedures for this simulation are described below.

Procedures/Materials: Form a large circle with all members standing facing one another. Large groups (60+) can be divided and asked to form two smaller circles. Provide a soft ball about the size of a volleyball for participants to work with. (Each circle would need a ball to work with.)

Goal: The object of the simulation is to keep the ball in the air for as long as it takes for each member of the team to touch the ball at least one time. Count the number of hits on the ball and try to beat the previous record each time the ball is put into play after it has fallen to the ground.

Rules: The ball may not be held at any time. Each person can hit the ball as many times as necessary throughout the game, but individuals may not at any point hit the ball consecutively. If the ball touches the ground, it is considered out of play and the counting starts over.

Facilitation: After three minutes of play allow the group five minutes to discuss and plan their strategy for success. If needed, allow planning to occur after each additional three to five minutes of play until the group reaches its goal or at least beats its highest record.

Debrief: Use the questions in Chart 1.1 to debrief the simulation with the group. The right-hand column of the chart provides you with some target responses that you are hoping to pull out from participants in response to the questions posed.

Chart 1.1

Question	*Target Responses to Pull From Team*
What did we need to do as a group to be successful?	Work collaboratively and cooperate Communicate Remain flexible and open to new ideas Plan and take risks Participate
What helped us reach our goal?	Planning Communication Trying new ideas
What made reaching our goal challenging?	Poor communication Individuals or groups working independently from the group Confusion/lack of direction
How does this simulation relate to the work we do at our site?	Need for planning and clarity of focus Collaboration and cooperation are critical to meet all students' needs Everyone must be on board and willing to try new things and take risks Direction must be clear and planning must be part of the process to reach success

Simulations such as Moon Ball can serve the purpose of setting the stage for the need for staff members to accept and embrace new ways to work together in order to improve communication and collaboration. They give them a viable rationale for actively participating in various groupings and processes as a staff when handling site-based challenges.

Hallways and Community Areas

 The first impression formed by staff, students, and visitors occurs immediately upon entering a facility. In some cases, it happens even before an individual leaves the parking lot! Maintaining a clean and orderly environment sends a very clear message that school is a place for serious work!

A building engineer or custodian should be directed to regularly clean and maintain student lockers, restrooms, cafeteria tables, and outdoor equipment to keep them free from graffiti and in safe working order at all times. Some find it helpful to walk through the building at the beginning of the year with the lead custodian or engineer to identify areas or items in need of attention or replacement. In addition, you may wish to sit down with this individual to outline your expectations for building maintenance and cleaning so that he or she can have the opportunity to share ideas and clarify personal responsibilities.

Organization is critical to success for students, staff, and leaders. Hallways should be free of clutter, and rooms and community areas should be properly labeled so they can be located quickly and easily. Students should be aware of where to find the lost-and-found box, where lockers and locker rooms are located, where lunch boxes should be left in the cafeteria, and which doors to exit and enter from during the school day.

Common areas used by all members of the community, such as the media center and technology lab, should be properly maintained and organized to allow for efficient use of materials. A simple example relates to the use of the technology lab in a school. Lab times should be posted on the lab door so both teachers and students are aware of the schedule. This organizational tool can be helpful in the event that technology needs arise during the school day and additional lab time is needed. Without having to track down the technology manager for the building, a teacher or students themselves at the secondary level can simply check the schedule and sign up for an open spot.

Finally, clear processes and procedures for moving throughout the building should be explained, reviewed, and upheld during the school year. An enormous amount of time can be wasted if students talking excessively in the hallway disturb other classrooms, or if staff members are searching a building looking for a student who left a classroom without a pass for study hall or the restroom. If students are on a closed campus, then those found outdoors should be questioned as to their destination and taken into the facility for direction. Behaviors that are expected need to be modeled and reinforced by all adults in order for them to be upheld throughout a school, and practices should be put in place to effectively monitor school rules and procedures. Setting up procedures for assigning hall monitors in secondary schools or student safety patrols at the elementary level may be an effective way to maintain order within the halls and common areas during the school day. The regular scheduling and overseeing of these student monitors is a task that can be turned over to a guidance team, a counselor, or an upper-level teacher.

Chapter Review

Even the most unorganized of individuals can develop systems to create an aura of organization around him or her. It is important to remember that organization goes far beyond an individual's personal office space, although that is a critical starting point. Effectively utilizing files and having a plan in place for efficiently managing information going in and out of a leader's office is critical to surviving in a leadership role. Beyond the office, it is important for a leader to put systems in place for saving precious time around conducting building meetings. Finally, designing and maintaining an organized work facility that includes all community areas can and will save everyone an enormous amount of time and stress.

Chapter 2

Organization of
Time

Time is not an endless resource, but rather it is a limited and sacred gift that cannot be bought, borrowed, or stolen. The sooner we accept this simple fact, the quicker we will commit to changing our habits and developing sound systems designed to increase our own productivity and making the best use of the precious amount of time that we are given each day. Identifying the systems is child's play in comparison to actually changing personal habits. Yet, the motivation of saving two to three hours of time on average each day may be enough to thrust most into a brand-new world governed by personal management of time. Robert Ramsey (1999), in his book *Lead, Follow or Get Out of the Way*, supports this philosophy of self-management of time when he writes, "It doesn't take any more knowledge to use time wisely—just more will." This chapter introduces a variety of simple tools and strategies for leaders to implement in an effort to make the best use of their daily work time. In addition, tips for effectively managing long-range projects are addressed. Although all the strategies have been tested in the field and found to increase productivity and save time, they are meant to be revised and adapted in order to best fit the individual needs of the user.

Getting Organized From the Start

One of the most important keys to effectively utilizing time is to organize repetitive yearly events right up front. At the close of one year, or the beginning of a new one, time can be wisely spent designing sign-up sheets for staff membership on various committees or participation in events that will occur at different times during the school year. This may include sign-ups for membership on schoolwide committees, coordinators for afterschool clubs, attendance at monthly PTA meetings, providing refreshments or snacks for professional development sessions, grade-level bulletin board displays, or department articles for parent newsletters. Although the organization of sign-up sheets takes a little bit of time up front, once initiated it is done for the year, and after the sheets are finalized and typed up, secretaries and leaders can refer to them throughout the year to generate reminders for individuals, teams, or departments. Reminders to those who have signed up for specific PTA meetings or agreed to bring snacks for a special meeting can actually be inputted into an electronic calendar at the start of the year, and then they simply appear each week on the calendar just like magic. A little bit of time up front will ensure that tasks get done on time, and individuals will greatly appreciate the timely reminders. This topic of staff reminders will also be addressed in Chapter 4 under Staff Bulletins.

Setting up a personal calendar, either electronic or in paper form, at the beginning of the year is another time-saving tip for the new leader. Dates and times for district meetings are most often generated and sent out to leaders at the beginning of the school year. These dates and times for the year should be placed on the calendar when they are disseminated. By doing this in advance, long-term projects can be plotted out, and building activities and events can also be scheduled for the year without the worry of conflicts. Below is a listing of some of the building meetings and events that should be scheduled at the beginning of the year and distributed to staff through a staff handbook.

Staff Meetings

Parent Advisor/Accountability Committee Meetings

Parent Teacher Association Meetings

Leadership Team Meetings

Grade-Level/Department Meetings

Classified/Supervision Team Meetings (Paraprofessionals, Teacher Aides)

Support Team Meetings (Guidance Counselors, Student Deans, etc.)

Professional Development Sessions (Inservices or Training sessions)

Parent Teacher Conferences

Office Staff Meetings

Special School Activities/Events (e.g., Field Day, Concerts, Literacy Nights, Theater Productions). These events should also be inputted into the weekly electronic calendar at the start of the school year for reference in the future.

Sporting Events (These are probably best left to each coach to develop and distribute separately due to the large number of games, tournaments, etc., involved.)

Leaders who are involved in monitoring and evaluating staff members should also consider generating a yearly observation and evaluation calendar to keep them on top of these critical events and to ensure that the events are spread out in a manageable manner throughout the school year. As the schedule is developed for the school year, make sure to take into account short weeks that are embedded for holidays and staff inservice days, and plan accordingly. Also, make sure to allow yourself one to two weeks to complete a formal written evaluation. This way, if you run behind you still can complete your task prior to your own established deadline. If you do feel that you need more time to complete an evaluation, make sure to communicate this need to the staff members, as they will be anticipating that you will honor your own schedule. A sample schedule has been provided as reference (Chart 2.1).

Once observation/evaluation schedules are developed and distributed to those involved, the task of setting up the specific date and time for an observation and related conferences should be left to the individual being observed. These folks should be asked to touch base with you at least one week in advance of their scheduled observation week to set up dates and times that will work. Setting up the preobservation conference, the observation time itself, and the post conference all at once will save everyone time later on. As individuals schedule their observations and conferences, it may help to check them off on a master observation/evaluation schedule so that you

Chart 2.1

> **Century Elementary School**
> **Certificated Observation/Evaluation Schedule**
> **1999-2000 school year**
>
> In order to ensure that staff members be observed and evaluated according to the Aurora Public Schools' guidelines, the following observation/evaluation conference schedule has been developed. Please see me at least one week prior to your scheduled Observation Week in order to arrange for times and dates for your observation. A pre- and post-observation conference will also be scheduled. Allow the following amounts of time for conferences and observations:
>
> Pre-observation
> Conference: 20-30 minutes   Observation: 30-40 minutes
>
> Post-observation
> Conference: 45-60 minutes   Evaluation Conference: 20-30 minutes
>
> This schedule is NOT set in stone. If a week doesn't work well for you simply see me to make an adjustment. (O - observation, E - evaluation)
>
> First Semester
>
> | Week | Staff Observation | Staff Evaluation Conferences |
> |------|-------------------|------------------------------|
> | September 13 | Carleton (O 1)
MacHendrie (O 1) | |
> | September 20 | Kuhn (O 1)
Davis (O 1) | |
> | September 27 | Burnham (O 1)
Mulqueen (O 1) | |
> | October 11 | Canipe (O 1) | |
> | October 18 | Carleton (O 2)
MacHendrie (O 2) | |
> | November 8 | Kuhn (O 2) | Carleton (E 1) |
> | November 15 | Davis (O 2)
Borom (O 1) | |
> | November 22 | | Kuhn (E 1) |
> | November 29 | Burnham (O 2)
Burns (O 1) | MacHendrie (E 1) |
> | December 6 | McGahey (O 1)
Meschko (O 1) | Davis (E 1) |
> | December 13 | | Burnham (E 1) |

can stay on top of the schedule and not get behind. Likewise, as formal evaluations are written and conferences held, these can also be marked off on the master observation/evaluation schedule. Once conducted, observation notes and summaries and evaluations should be filed in the confidential personnel files

> *"Whereas many managers run out of time,*
> *real leaders run into time*
> *by finding ways to do things*
> *better, quicker, more efficiently, or not at all."*
>
> Robert D. Ramsey

Appointments and Messages

Many individuals with whom you will work will make the assumption that at the same time you earned your title of Assistant Principal or Principal you also gave up complete control over your time during your day. They assume that their concerns and issues take precedence over anything else that may be on your calendar. You will come to realize that everyone wants a piece of your time, and usually they want it RIGHT NOW! Ramsey writes, "Time management is simply making choices. Better choices mean better time use. Effective school leaders make the right choices more often than most people do. It starts by determining who's boss when it comes to time."

Fortunately, with a little bit of planning and stamina, a new leader has the ability to take some of this control back into his or her own hands, and it can be done in such a way as to not offend those who come knocking determined to see you immediately.

Teachers have planning periods during which they can return phone calls or meet personally with parents, and the rest of their time is dedicated to teaching children. In other words, they have prioritized their time and put their students first. This philosophy is generally understood and accepted by parents, students, staff, and community members. As a school leader, you also should put children first. This means dedicating the majority of your time to meeting the needs of children through coaching and mentoring staff, overseeing the implementation of programs, handling safety issues and school discipline, managing school finances, planning professional development opportunities for staff, and monitoring long-range plans. As a school administrator your classroom is much larger than those of your teachers and explaining this concept to your community right from the beginning will provide you with the necessary justification for maintaining weekly office hours.

Office hours are simply hours dedicated throughout the week during which you are available to meet with parents who have concerns, to return phone calls, and to handle staff issues that are not of an urgent nature. It is important that you schedule office hours daily initially, when possible, and reserve this time for handling just the issues mentioned previously. An hour block per day should be more than adequate. You may want to consider alternating your times between morning and afternoon in order to accommodate varying schedules. Communicating this schedule to your secretary and office staff on a weekly basis will keep them informed and allow them to efficiently schedule appointments for you during designated times. In addition, they will be able to communicate to those who simply desire a return phone call an approximate time of when they will be hearing back from you.

Communicating this procedure to parents and community members through a monthly newsletter is critical if it is to be accepted in a positive manner, and don't forget to include your rationale for setting up such a system. Also, you may wish to include who in the office they should speak with to schedule a time during your office hours, so they are provided with the name or names of one or more individuals to contact. Of course, you have to remain flexible and attend to emergencies or urgent matters immediately. The key is to discern which of the issues that arise require your immediate attention and which you can handle in a less urgent fashion. Optimally, if you can meet with your secretary on a daily basis to set out your priorities for the day, both of you will have a better idea of what time you have available. On many days your schedule may allow you to address parental or staff issues as they arise, which is ultimately the best for everyone. This option will be more palatable for those who prefer more of an open door policy, but it is important for everyone to realize that on some days this simply may not be realistic.

If you choose to opt for the office hour approach, you will find that most of the days your allotted time will be open, which will allow you flexibility in how to use the time. After six months on the job, you will have a better idea of just how much time you need to routinely schedule for office hours. You may find one hour, two days a week, to be sufficient.

First Things First

"I am personally persuaded that the essence of the best thinking in the area of time management can be captured in a single phrase: Organize and execute around priorities."

Stephen R. Covey

Chart 2.2   Prioritizing Tasks

MUST DO	SHOULD DO	WOULD BE NICE	WAITING TO HEAR
Email 5th re: DARE	October Newsletter 9/15	Book study survey	Assessment schedule
Meeting Agenda 9/4	PTA fundraiser memo		Wagers signed evaluation
Tom M behavior slip			

Prioritizing tasks is the key to using time wisely and increasing productivity. A simple work chart, like the one depicted in Chart 2.2, is an effective tool for managing both short- and long-term tasks.

When the chart is enlarged to fit on a piece of 11" x 8½" paper, small sticky notes fit perfectly within each of the columns. Instead of making a list of items on a sheet of paper, simply place tasks on sticky notes. Then prioritize each task based on deadlines and stick them on the appropriate column on the chart. You may wish to include a due date right on the sticky note as a reminder to yourself as to when tasks need to be completed.

Each of the columns is assigned a different level of priority. The Must Do section of the chart is for high priority tasks. The other columns are best used for smaller tasks that are a part of a larger, more long-range project or for those tasks that do not have a close approaching deadline. Often tasks move from one column to the next, as priorities change. When a task is completed, the note is removed from the chart and discarded. The final column of the chart is reserved for tasks that require a response from a third party. This final column could also be used as a reminder column for you to check on a task delegated to another employee. The final column of activities could also be placed within what is known as a "tickler" file. This is a file containing items that you would review on a weekly or monthly basis. If you review items in the tickler file regularly, you will be able to keep abreast of projects that are being carried out by others and make any necessary follow-up calls or set debriefing meetings.

It may be helpful for a leader to assist an office staff member or secretary in setting up a monthly tickler file to stay ahead on deadlines and project due dates. Leaders will learn that each month specific tasks will need to be completed by the school office, many of which can be handled by an office staff member or secretary. Some of the items that are appropriate for the secretary's tickler file are listed below; as the year progresses additional tasks appropriate to this file will be passed on to site leaders:

- Attendance reports
- Discipline tracking reports
- Monthly newsletter items
- Staffing reports
- Schedule changes for the month (reminders may need to be generated to appropriate personnel)
- Grant funding reports

By meeting with office personnel and/or a secretary on a weekly basis, you can discuss the items coming up in the next month, clarify tasks to be completed, and develop time lines for longer projects collaboratively.

Long-Range Projects

Each school year a leader will complete several long-range projects that require additional organization and prioritization of tasks. So often, leaders put off long-range projects until the last minute. This can cause undue stress on the leader as well as those around him or her who are called upon to complete tasks with minimum time. Having an organized system in place for attacking long-range projects may assist a leader in getting started earlier and avoiding the panic and chaos brought on by procrastination. As long-range projects are assigned it is important to break them apart or task-analyze them in order to delineate the various subtasks associated with the end product. Once these subtasks are identified a leader will need to sequence them according to an appropriate order for task completion, assign reasonable deadlines for each, and finally identify who will be responsible for the subtasks. Many times subtasks can be divided among a team of individuals, making a large project more manageable. The planning form in Chart 2.3 provides a template for organizing long-range projects.

Chart 2.3

Long-Range Project Planning Form

Project Title:		
Project Outcome(s):		
Project Due Date:		
Submit To:		
Subtasks:	Completion Deadline	Person Responsible

Chart 2.4

Task:
_____

_____

Due Date:
_____

Details:
_____

_____

_____

_____

_____

Completion Date:
_____

Location of Original:
_____

_____

Subtasks and due dates can be added to a leader's priority chart or placed within a secretary's monthly tickler file for completion. Completed long-range project planning forms should be placed in a file folder housed in the second shelf of the set of four stackable shelves. As subtasks associated with a larger project are completed, they can be placed directly in the file folder. If various subtasks are assigned out to others, these file folders, along with the original planning forms, can be reviewed on a regular basis to check on progress. In addition, a leader may wish to have a secretary or other individual to whom work has been delegated submit a simple task completion form along with the completed subtask. A form such as the one provided in Chart 2.4 will help keep a leader on top of tasks that have been assigned to others.

This simple task completion form can also be used for short-term tasks assigned to others. Once subtasks have been submitted, reviewed, and finalized, the specific subtask can be checked off by the leader on the original project planning form.

Chapter Review

The key to effective organization is setting up organizational systems right in the beginning. Designing calendars and sign-up charts for key events and activities that will take place throughout the year will save a leader time later on in the school year. In addition, it is important for a leader to take control over his or her personal time by planning ahead and putting systems in place for managing appointments and meetings. Prioritizing tasks on a daily basis will enable a leader to stay on top of and complete managerial tasks ahead of imposed deadlines. Finally, the management of long-range projects is crucial to leadership success. Planning forms and task completion sheets can be helpful to a leader in identifying subtasks related to long-term projects. Planning and setting deadlines for subtasks will enable a leader to more efficiently manage long-range projects.

> *"Time management is really a misnomer—*
> *the challenge is not to manage time,*
> *but to manage ourselves."*
>
> Stephen R. Covey

Chapter 3

Organization of
Programs

Maintaining the philosophy of "children first" results in a need for effective organization of building programs. This chapter focuses on key strategies for ensuring that organizational programming occurs in such a manner as to achieve quality results. Under this heading of programming, the following issues will be addressed:

Developing schedules to allow for learning blocks,

Creating learning expectations for levels or courses,

Establishing effective methods for monitoring student progress toward identified goals,

Designing professional development to meet needs of personnel, and

Monitoring staff to ensure quality instruction.

Developing Learning Blocks

As education begins to embrace the new era of information and technology, it is critical that schools begin to look more critically at how students spend their time in school. Our current society demands that students develop higher-level thinking skills related to locating and processing information, evaluating knowledge, and drawing conclusions from a vast amount of data. In order to effectively develop these types of learning skills, large blocks of consistent instruction are necessary. Thus, there is a need for reevaluating current educational schedules and making a shift to longer interrelated learning blocks for students of all ages.

Over the course of the past 10 years, middle schools across the country began to look at and implement block scheduling in order to meet just this need. Elementary schools, which have historically departmentalized subjects into short learning periods, have also started to take a more thoughtful look at how their time with students is scheduled. Even departments at the high school level have begun to investigate ways to maximize student instruction by designing learning opportunities across various disciplines to allow students to more readily apply their learning in various arenas. Teachers have found that by integrating key subject areas, such as reading, writing, and mathematics, across the curriculum and extending the learning time into longer, more integrated blocks, they are able to accomplish more with students than they had previously when learning time was broken up throughout the day into small chunks of time.

Research surrounding best practices has revealed that students who are provided with longer instructional blocks on a regular basis perform better on standardized assessments. Longer instructional blocks provide teachers with the necessary time to extend learning and delve deeper into concepts. This ensures students a strong foundation upon which to build. This deep learning simply was not possible in our previous scheduling system where teachers and students were forced to completely switch gears every 30 to 50 minutes in order to ensure that all content was covered.

For elementary school leaders, it is imperative that scheduling of learning blocks takes precedence over other building activities. When a school states that they provide students with an "uninterrupted literacy block," for example, it is up to the leader to make sure that that time block is sacred. *Uninterrupted* means that students and teachers are left to work during those identified time frames. All other building activities must be scheduled around the set learning blocks.

Ultimately, the leader is the one responsible for ensuring that this does in fact happen. Some of the most common interruptions are listed below.

- Specials (Art, Music, P.E.)
- Assemblies
- Recess
- Computer time
- Guest speakers
- Drug awareness and resistance programs

By planning ahead and making thoughtful decisions regarding scheduling, learning blocks truly can be "uninterrupted." At the elementary level, students should have two extended learning blocks. One identified as a literacy block (1½-3 hours) and one targeted on mathematics (1-1½ hours).

In most schools, primary grades are scheduled to have their literacy block in the morning, leaving the math block to occur in the afternoon. Intermediate grades are scheduled in just the opposite manner, with the math block scheduled in the morning and literacy in the afternoon. This type of schedule allows for intermediate grades to have content studies, specials, recesses, or assemblies during the morning either before or after the math block and primary grades to have these other activities in the afternoon.

At the middle school level, the scheduling of learning blocks may find you treading some uncomfortable ground with teachers. Historically these individuals have taught in teams where individuals were solely responsible for only one or maybe two content areas and students moved from one teacher to the next for 50-minute periods. Implementing more of a block schedule requires teachers to become more integrated in their teaching, and they may even need to work outside of their designated field of study.

If teachers are paired to provide the primary content instruction, the longer block scheduling system can be implemented effectively at the middle school level. One of the pair would be responsible for teaching students literacy and social studies, for example, while the teammate would provide instruction in math and science. Of course, some literacy components would be naturally embedded into the content area block, and topic studies related to science may be found in the literacy block. This integration would require teammates to work in a collaborative manner and engage in regular planning, effective communication, and sharing of materials and knowledge.

Once again, the leader would need to monitor and oversee the development of a block schedule system in order to ensure that all students were provided with uninterrupted learning blocks during the day. Students would need to be scheduled for two learning blocks of 1½-2 hours each, per day. One block would be designated for literacy and social studies while the other would be focused on math and science. Elective courses, assemblies, and special events would again be scheduled around these longer, sacred time blocks.

Although scheduling to put learning blocks into place can be a challenge, it definitely makes for a wiser use of time for students throughout the school year. The initial investment of time to arrange for learning blocks will naturally occur when the system is put into place for the first time. Once designed, the schedule will be a model for future years and can often be reused after minor adjustments are made.

For high school leaders, schedules can be adjusted to allow for longer periods for more in-depth study. But the most important difference that can be appropriately implemented at this level is to provide opportunities for members from different departments to meet and discuss how concepts can be supported within all disciplines. With some collaboration, algebra teachers can discover ways to support biology instructors and speech teachers can support western civilization or foreign language instructors. As soon as teachers begin to communicate across disciplines the door to creativity is opened and the ideas can begin to flow. The key to seeing how disciplines can support one another is in identifying and establishing clear outcomes or expectations for courses or disciplines so that overlaps can be easily identified.

Learning Expectations

The educational arena today is marked by high stakes accountability for students, teachers, and leaders. State mandated assessments have become a major driving force for funding, programming, and how time is spent in the classroom. In an effort to design equitable measurement tools, states have developed educational standards and districts have followed suit by taking state standards and meshing them with their own unique systems, layered with outcomes, proficiencies, benchmarks, and exit criteria. Simply put, states, districts, and sites have spent a great deal of time determining exactly what students should be able to do, and at what point during their educational career.

The identification of learning expectations is critical to increasing student achievement at all levels. Students can't hit a mark they can't see or don't know is there. The expectations, if they are written in a clear and understandable manner, can be used as a guide for teachers as to where they need to head with students and how disciplines can be integrated. If managed correctly, they can also serve as the glue that holds school programs together in a seamless and cohesive manner. The key to their effectiveness lies in how they are developed, disseminated, and monitored. The leader's direction, vision, and support regarding the use of learning expectations directly impacts their effectiveness in raising student achievement. There are four key pieces to keep in mind in the development of learning expectations. First, it is critical that teachers work together, in a collaborative manner, in the development of the expectations. Second, the expectations should be based on state and/or national standards, where applicable. Third, expectations must be specific, clear, and measurable. Finally, there should be a natural flow from one level of expectations to the next. In other words, they should build upon one another without being repetitive.

Staff members need to work together to develop learning expectations for their level or discipline that are meaningful and clear. Also, cross-grade or discipline-level teams need to meet in order to make sure that expectations are in alignment with one another and that they naturally progress in difficulty from one level to the next without duplication. Leaders need to ensure that time is set aside for this important work to take place. In addition, once the expectations are developed, time for review, reflection, and revision should be part of a professional development plan to occur at the end of each school year.

In designing learning expectations, teams should begin by looking first at national and state standards, district proficiencies or expectations, and other level expectations that have been developed by other schools or districts. These documents will serve as a wonderful beginning point for teams. Often these standards are ambiguous and unclear, and because they have not had a stake in their development, teachers fail to buy into the importance of using them as a guide in their classrooms. Just the discussion surrounding the standards will move teachers to a higher level of understanding and will increase their comfort level with them.

When looking at the standards or other documents, teams should first identify items that are already clear and understandable and then reword, adjust, or simplify the language of other items to develop a list of expectations that are specific, measurable, and achievable for students at their level. Teachers need to determine what strategies and skills the average students at their grade level should be proficient in by the end of the school year or course term. It is important to avoid using words such as *partially, sometimes,* or *begins to* within the learning expectations as these concepts are difficult to measure.

Drafts should be shared with cross-grade-level teams and/or among different discipline teams. The goal of these discussions should be to make sure that the expectations progress from one level to the next, to eliminate duplications, and to identify where disciplines can support one another. If two levels have both identified the same skill or strategy, generally it should be eliminated from the higher level, and replaced by a skill or strategy that is more challenging.

Once a draft of level expectations is developed, teams can work together to determine an appropriate time frame for teaching and assessing the specific skills. Dividing the expectations among quarters, trimesters, or semesters will provide teams with a long-range plan for instruction. Providing teams with a simple planning tool, such as the forms in Chart 3.1 or Chart 3.2, will expedite this process, and once completed it can be typed into a spread sheet to create an assessment monitoring checklist.

Teachers should work together as a school to determine how the assessment sheets will be marked. Most often a checklist such as this is assessed using a basic system such as:

+	Exceeds Expectation
v	Meets Expectation
x	Partially Meets Expectation
—	Does Not Meet Expectation

In addition, each column on the chart could be divided into two or three columns to allow for multiple assessments of the same expectation. This provides an opportunity for students to demonstrate the development of skills over time.

Although the above example is from an elementary grade, the same process and table can be adapted to be used at both the middle school and high school level to ensure consistent learning targets and ongoing assessment of student progress within various disciplines.

Monitoring Student Progress

The most effective way for leaders to directly impact student achievement is through monitoring progress on a regular basis. Collecting

Chart 3.1   4th Grade Level Expectations—Reading

Period	Expectation	Assessment Tool
1st Quarter	*Applies knowledge and understanding of similes to gain meaning from text	Writing journal or Reading response log
	*Uses homophones to gain meaning when reading	Reading response log
	*Retells text and includes characters, setting, plot, and events that lead to solution	Individual reading assessment—oral retell
	*Uses drama or music to illustrate an understanding of sensory images presented in a text	Teacher observation or Student self-evaluation
2nd Quarter	*Attends to apostrophes for possession	Running record form
	*Attends to commas and adjusts pace accordingly	Running record form
	*Makes text-to-text connections and explains how the connection assisted him or her in developing understandings of what is read	Reading response log
	*Identifies two viewpoints in a text	Reading response log or Venn diagram

and analyzing schoolwide student achievement data will provide a leader with the necessary information to make informed decisions regarding programming and professional development needs for staff. It also opens up the door to speak with staff members regarding building trends, students' needs, and effectiveness of instructional strategies being used.

Once teams have identified level expectations for critical content areas (reading, writing, and math at the elementary and middle school level, and specific disciplines such as biology, algebra, literature, etc., at the high school level) and designed a long-range plan for instruction and assessment of those expectations, the next step is to design an assessment schedule for buildingwide data collection, analysis, and follow through.

Data collection, analysis, and follow-through can end up taking an enormous amount of time if they are not conducted in a systematic

Chart 3.2   1st Quarter Reading Learning Expectations (4th Grade)

Students	Applies knowledge and understanding of similes to gain meaning	Uses homophones to gain meaning	Retells text and includes characters, setting, plot, and events leading to a solution	Uses drama or music to illustrate an understanding of sensory images presented in a text

Assessment Monitoring Checklist

manner. The key to making this important task manageable is to have a realistic plan in place for handling it, designing and distributing an assessment schedule at the start of the school year and sticking to it!

Planning for data collection, analysis, and follow-through involves designing collection methods and tools and scheduling time for critical events either individually or with a leadership team. In the beginning of the year it is critical for you to sit down with members

Chart 3.3

Level	Total Number of Students	Number Meeting or Exceeding Expectations	Percentage Meeting or Exceeding Expectations
Sixth			
Seventh			
Eighth			
Building Total			

of your leadership team and determine how building results will be tabulated and ask your secretary to design a basic form to be used monthly to record results. For example, if you are gathering and analyzing student achievement toward level expectations, you might decide to look at the number of students from each grade level who met or exceeded all of the designated criteria for that assessment period. If this were the case, a simple form such as the one in Chart 3.3 would work beautifully in assimilating building results.

Of course, this form would not provide you with much information regarding specific grade level data or students' needs. To gain more specific data from a specific level, a form such as the one in Chart 3.4 would be more informative.

The form in Chart 3.4 could also be used to collect data from individual staff members on student progress toward meeting identified learning expectations. Using a more detailed form, such as this, will provide you with more in-depth information related to student progress within each individual classroom or within specific courses. In addition, these data can give you insight into classroom progress and professional development needs for individual teachers and assist you in identifying teachers who might be able to serve as a resource for others in developing a specific skill or strategy with students. (The communication between teammates surrounding monthly data will be discussed in the Empowerment section of this text.)

Once it has been determined what data will be collected, how they will be tabulated for analysis, and appropriate forms have been developed, it is important to schedule dates for data collection. If assessment data are to be used to drive instructional practice and determine

Chart 3.4

Fourth Grade 1st Quarter Expectations	Total Number of Students	Total Number Meeting or Exceeding Expectations	Percentage Meeting or Exceeding Expectations
Applies knowledge and understanding of similes			
Uses homophones to gain meaning when reading			
Retells text and includes characters, setting, plot, and events leading to solution			
Uses drama or music to illustrate an understanding of sensory images presented in text			

professional development needs of staff, then it is essential that they be collected on a regular basis throughout the school year. Working collaboratively with a leadership team and staff to determine the frequency of data collection will increase the buy-in of those involved. (A discussion surrounding the development and purpose of a leadership teams can be found in Chapter 8.) Most often teams find that collecting and analyzing building data on a quarterly basis is reasonable and effective. Individual teams should most definitely be involved in more frequent data collection and analysis, but this will occur through the implementation of team or department meetings, which will be discussed in the Empowerment section of this text.

Optimally, data collection dates should be determined at the beginning of the school year and a list of these essential dates should be distributed to staff. These dates should also be placed on the yearly electronic calendar along with reminders a week in advance. In addition, a short note about assessment due dates in a staff bulletin will give staff one more chance to be aware of deadlines in advance. Although designing the schedule in advance and making sure to put reminder notes on calendars and in bulletins takes time, it will save a leader an enormous amount of time in the end, when data are actually submitted on time and in the format requested.

Meeting dates and times for leadership teams to analyze building data should also be set once assessment collection dates have been finalized. Placing these dates and times immediately on the calendar will save time later and ensure that these important meetings occur in a timely manner after data are collected. Make sure to allow at least one week between the date assessment data are due and the leadership team analysis meeting. This will provide adequate time for data to be tabulated prior to the analysis meeting. At the conclusion of each data analysis meeting, strategies for sharing results with staff should be discussed. Results may be discussed at team or department meetings or during a full staff meeting, or they may be published in a staff bulletin. Regardless of the format for dissemination, it is critical that the team determine the process to be used and follow through on the sharing in a timely manner. Otherwise, staff will begin to lose interest and may view the data as trivial and of low priority.

Collecting data from staff can be a cumbersome task, but with some advance preparation and planning it can be done efficiently and effectively. Work with your secretary to create a data collection folder to be used each month when data are to be gathered. A staff roster containing only the names of those who will be turning in data should be placed inside the folder and used as a check off sheet as information is submitted to the office. All data collected should remain in this folder until it is complete and ready for analysis. Once all data are collected, the entire folder is passed along to the leader or the individual in charge of tabulating the data for the month.

Staff members have a tendency to become overwhelmed and frustrated when they are kept in the dark about assessment procedures. When this occurs, they lose sight of how important the data can be to providing a quality instructional program for students. Determining what data are to be collected, when they will be due, and how they will be shared will assist the leader in efficiently managing this critical task and keeping staff members on board with maintaining an effective system of using assessment to drive instruction throughout the building.

Professional Development Plans

In gathering data from case studies, Michael Fullan concludes, "Professional development or training of individuals or even of small teams will not be sufficient. For this reason schools must also focus on creating schoolwide professional learning communities." One way to accomplish this goal is to design professional development plans for staff based on analysis of schoolwide student achievement data. By looking at student assessment data, a leader can determine specific areas that are in need of improvement. It is important to maintain the attitude that if students aren't achieving, staff members need additional support in providing effective instruction to help them learn. For example, if assessment data show that students are consistently failing to gain meaning from complex vocabulary, then it may be appropriate to provide staff with research-based strategies for handling vocabulary. If analysis of students' writing data shows that students have minimal understanding of how to organize their writing to effectively communicate their thoughts, then professional development time focused on organizational strategies for writing might be the perfect next step. If foreign language students are falling short of the expectations related to oral language proficiency, then support is needed related to strategies for increasing students' oral language fluency. The key is to correlate student data to staff needs and design a plan for improving instruction in identified areas in order to increase student achievement.

Determining Needs

Analyzing end-of-year school data is often the most efficient means for establishing building trends and identifying staff needs for professional development. A multitude of needs will come to light from the analysis of end-of-year data. By categorizing the needs, a differentiated plan for professional development will begin to take shape. Identified areas should be placed into categories as follows:

Buildingwide Needs: These are areas that consistently appear across all levels and disciplines within a building.

Grade-Level/Team/Department Needs: These are areas that fall out as a need at a particular level, among a team, or within a specific discipline such as natural sciences.

Individual Needs: These are needs that stand out in a couple of small groups of children across a building. Generally, these will be discussed with individual teachers or teams rather than shared with the entire staff.

Prioritizing Needs

Once needs are determined and categorized, the next step is to prioritize the needs. A building leadership team or the full staff should be directly involved in prioritizing a building's professional development needs. Buildingwide needs should be prioritized first under the following headings:

Must Do	Should Do	Would Be Nice

Chart paper and sticky notes can be used to categorize needs efficiently within each of the categories mentioned. Each heading is placed on a separate piece of chart paper and posted in the front of the room where everyone can see it. Next, write the identified needs on individual sticky notes and ask an individual in the group to begin by placing each of the notes on the charts according to where he or she feels they fall in regard to priority. As the notes are placed, the individual is required to provide the group with a verbal rationale for why items are being placed under specific priority categories. Once all of the items are placed on the charts, other group members are asked if there are any they wish to move. Staff members are allowed to move an item to a different category providing that they can verbalize a rationale to the group. The process continues until all group members are satisfied with the way the items are prioritized.

Establishing Time Frames for Implementation

Establishing realistic time frames to cover professional development needs is the next step in the process. Record an approximate amount of time needed to cover each of the professional development items directly on the individual sticky notes. Time frames will range from a full day's inservice to a 50-minute staff meeting, and can even be several 50-minute staff meeting sessions over the course of the year. Keep in mind that these initial time frames may need to be adjusted as planning for individual professional development topics begins.

The final step in the prioritizing process involves designing a yearlong plan for implementation. This step is usually done most effectively with a small group of individuals, such as a leadership team or professional development task force. The group will first need to determine all time frames throughout the year that can be used for professional development opportunities. In most cases this would include full- and half-day inservices; after school professional development sessions; staff meetings; and grade-level, team, or department meetings. Items are scheduled into time blocks in order to allow for all members who were directly related to the need initially to participate. This may mean that during a two-hour professional development time, three different activities may be occurring at once. The result is the development of a differentiated professional development plan based on staff needs as dictated by student achievement data. Once completed, the plan—including dates, session topics, and outcomes—should be compiled and distributed to staff. An example depicting a semester-long plan for professional development is included in Chart 3.5. Of course semester-long professional development plans will vary depending on the needs of the individual site. In many cases, it may be unrealistic for team or department meetings to be held simultaneously. It is more likely that each individual team will schedule monthly meetings to fit its own schedule.

Monitoring Staff

Regular monitoring of individual staff members is a critical piece in ensuring that programs are implemented effectively, time is used wisely, and continuity exists between levels and across disciplines. Some certificated staff members will be monitored throughout the school year in order to satisfy state and district requirements. This section addresses the regular monitoring of all staff members within a site, rather than just those on the formal evaluation cycle.

For the most part, states and districts will provide an administrator with a process for formally observing and evaluating certificated staff members. In most states, certificated staff members participate in a formal observation and evaluation process throughout their probationary years. The probationary period ranges from two to four years, depending on the state. In addition, nonprobationary staff members are also scheduled to be on formal observation every two to three years. Specific guidelines related to frequency and duration of observations, as well as time lines for completing formal evaluations of certificated staff members, will be provided to the administrator and for the most part must be followed as stated.

All staff members within a site should be informally monitored each year on a regular basis by a building administrator or his or her designee. This may be an assistant principal, lead teacher, or site mentor. This task can be accomplished in an organized and systematic manner through the use of some very simple organizational forms and a well thought out system.

Record Keeping

Using a staff monitoring notebook can assist a leader in maintaining accurate records and keeping track of staff monitoring. In the

Chart 3.5

Session Date/Time	Format	Focus/Topic
August 16 8:00-3:15	Inservice Day	Investigations Math Training (8:00-11:30) Team Building—Building Community (12:30-3:15)
August 17 8:00-3:15	Inservice Day	Writing To, With, and By
September 7 8:05-9:00	Team Meeting	Review exit criteria, set goal(s) for next month, and determine assessment tool
September 12 8:05-9:00	Staff Meeting	Mosaic of Thought Book Study Monitoring for Meaning (Read Intro, p. 44)
September 18 3:45-5:45	Afterschool Session	Writing Process—Forming Intentions and Developing Summary Statements
September 26 8:05-9:00	Staff Meeting	Writing Assessment—Analysis of Student Writing Samples
September 28 8:00-3:15	Inservice Day	Matchword Technology Training (8:00-11:30) Writing—Using data to determine small group instruction
October 12 8:05-9:00	Team Meeting	Share student data on set goal(s), share strategies used, identify goal for next month and assessment tool to be used
October 17 8:05-9:00	Staff Meeting	Mosaic of Thought Book Study Connecting Known to New (Read pp. 45-72)
October 19 8:00-3:15	Inservice Day	District Math Inservice OR Team Choice Professional Development
November 7 8:05-9:00	Staff Meeting	Writing Discussion—Process vs. Product
November 16 8:05-9:00	Team Meeting	Share student data on set goal(s), share strategies used, identify goal for next month and assessment tool to be used
November 19 3:45-5:45	Afterschool Session	Nonfiction Retelling—followed by ½ day training by level on Nov. 20
November 28 8:05-9:00	Staff Meeting	Mosaic of Thought Book Study Determining Importance (Read pp. 73-96)
December 14 8:05-9:00	Team Meeting	Share student data on set goal(s), share strategies used, identify goal for next month and assessment tool to be used
December 19 8:05-9:00	Staff Meeting	Writing Discussion—Mapping nonfiction by purpose and structure

front of a three-ring binder place an organizational chart with boxes adjusted to fit a small sticky note. Print the names of staff members in alphabetical order above each of the boxes. It may be helpful to keep certificated personnel separate from classified staff, but the system will work just as well if they are all together as long as they are listed in alphabetical order.

Behind the organizational chart in the binder, place a set of separation sheets with tabs labeled for each staff member, once again arranged in alphabetical order. Behind each tab there should be a few sheets of blank paper for posting notes on the individual staff members.

Once you have the binder set up you are ready to prepare for monitoring. Begin by placing a blank sticky note on top of each box on the organizational chart at the front of the notebook. As you observe a particular staff member you will make key notes on the sticky note placed on the box directly below the staff member's name. Make sure to place a date on the sticky note to identify when the observation took place. Once an informal observation is conducted and documented, the sticky note is removed from the organizational chart and adhered to the page directly behind the staff member's tab in the second part of the notebook. This will leave a blank space on the organizational chart that will visually alert you that an informal observation of that particular staff member has been recently documented.

Establish a goal for the regularity of informal observations you wish to conduct per staff member. Once every two or three weeks is probably realistic if you are working at this task individually. If you have a smaller site, or have support staff involved to assist in the monitoring, then weekly observations might be a realistic goal. Use the organizational chart as a visual guide to assist you in planning informal observations for the week and then schedule these on your personal task priority chart or on a calendar. Once all staff members have gone through a cycle of informal observations, the chart is refilled with sticky notes and the process starts over.

If you do have additional support staff assisting you in monitoring of staff members, it may work best to divide the staff members and place their information in separate binders. This way the individual observers can develop their own schedule for the group they are responsible for monitoring. Of course, you would want to regularly switch binders in order for the administrator to have ample opportunity to observe every staff member throughout the school year.

Sharing Observations

In order to share information with staff members regarding your findings and notes from informal observations you can easily make a photocopy of individual pages from the notebook. Keeping up with this on a monthly or quarterly basis will keep the lines of communication open between you and your staff members. Of course, if an observation raises a concern or stands out as being deserving of special recognition, you can always address it in a more immediate fashion.

Once you have completely filled a staff member's page in the binder, remove it, secure all the notes with clear tape, and place the page in the staff member's individual file. These informal monitoring notes can be a wonderful source of information when completing formal evaluations, even if the staff member is not due to be observed until the following year.

Clarifying Monitoring Goals

Identifying a clear goal or focus when conducting informal observations will also help to make regular monitoring more manageable. You may wish to discuss options with a leadership team and then jointly come up with one or two items to focus on as you monitor staff members. For example, if you are monitoring classified employees, you may be looking for their ability to use a specific problem-solving approach with students. Or, with certificated staff members, you may be looking for the implementation of the writing process throughout all curriculum areas. At the secondary level you may wish to focus on the integration of various content areas within courses. Having a clearly stated goal or focus for the observation will assist you in taking specific notes and will keep you on target with supporting staff in meeting identified school goals.

Monitoring goals or focus points should change periodically in order to allow you to keep abreast of what is occurring throughout your site in relation to the professional development plan, new programs and strategies being implemented, the overall morale of staff, and school climate.

Sharing your monthly or quarterly monitoring goals or focus points with staff will increase the trust level and will also send a clear message as to what you view as important. These goals can easily be shared through a staff bulletin. In addition, you may wish to recognize specific behaviors or examples related to your monitoring goal that you observe in classrooms. This type of recognition can also be placed in a staff bulletin and will provide staff with a small pat on the back for a job well done.

Chapter Review

Putting children first should always remain at the heart of the organization of building programs. Developing building schedules that allow for uninterrupted blocks of time for learning is the most fundamental of all pieces related to building programming. Once learning blocks are established, it is the leader's responsibility to support staff members in the development of clear learning expectations for grade levels, teams, and discipline teams. It is these expectations that will drive the instructional program and ensure learning at every level and continuity among levels and across content areas. Monitoring student progress toward established goals and expectations is the next step in ensuring an organized program designed to positively impact student achievement. Establishing regular intervals for gathering and analyzing student data will naturally lead to the development of a differentiated professional development plan for staff members. This plan will provide staff with the necessary tools to be successful in meeting the learning needs of all students. By implementing a system for regularly monitoring staff members, a leader can evaluate individual progress toward established building goals and provide staff with valuable input as to their performance.

Section II

Communication

Effective communication skills lie at the very heart of leadership. As a result, communication skills alone have the power to either make or break a leader. Communication involves both receiving as well as delivering information through verbal and nonverbal messages as well as written messages. Effective communicators have developed and refined their skills in listening, analyzing, and monitoring body behaviors to understand nonverbal messages and, of course, the art of written and oral discourse. Regardless of to whom the communication is being directed, or from whom it is being received, it is important to remember that communication is personal in nature, thus susceptible to interpretation. It is a multifaceted topic too often overlooked by new leaders until it is too late.

In order to communicate effectively, the leader must make sure that all communication is clear, honest, and straightforward. On the other side of the issue, it is also imperative that a leader have the necessary skills to effectively discern information communicated by others in such a way as to identify the main ideas, underlying truths, and bottom-line expectations. Although effective communication skills do come naturally to some, for others they take time, persistence, and a great deal of practice. Fortunately, the foundational skills related to communication highlighted previously can be taught, learned, and improved upon if the desire is there. For school leaders, there is truly no choice to make in this area. Communication skills are a must, thus they must be cultivated and developed in order for leaders to lead where others will follow. Robert Ramsey (1999) states, "One of the first rules of good communication is to get the attention of the intended receiver. This requires knowing who your exact audience is and how to reach it."

School leaders address a wide range of audiences on a daily basis; it is simply an inherent part of the position, but generally a leader communicates with three primary groups: building staff, parents and community members, and district personnel. Thus, this section on communication is divided into three chapters in which each of these primary audiences is addressed separately.

Chapter 4

Communicating With Building Staff

Building leaders communicate with staff throughout each and every day through nonverbal messages, written correspondence, and face-to-face interactions. Leaders who have taken the time to look closely at communication have learned that careful planning and preparation are the keys to making any form of communication effective. Thus, this chapter begins with a discussion surrounding planning and preparing for in-building communication, followed by a look at the most common forms of communication that occur within the walls of a school, including staff bulletins, e-mail messages, and meetings involving face-to-face interaction with staff members. Nonverbal forms of communication that often send the most powerful messages, but often receive the least amount of attention by building leaders, will be addressed next. The chapter concludes with a discussion surrounding genuine listening and group processing strategies.

Planning and Preparation

The first step to take in moving toward becoming a more effective communicator is to take the time to carefully plan the types of communication to be used and to make an estimate as to how often each type will be used. This analysis will lead to the development of a comprehensive communication plan that will assist you in staying in touch with your staff members, keeping them up to date on critical issues, and offering regular opportunities for staff to interact with you to share ideas, feedback, or concerns. As you begin to analyze the forms of communication that you plan to use, you will come to the realization that the need to identify the underlying purpose for the communication is of utmost importance. The type of communication you select will be driven by the outcome(s) you hope to achieve. For example, if you wish to gain feedback from staff members related to a new initiative being implemented in the building, then a face-to-face meeting may be the most appropriate choice, whereas a written bulletin may be the best vehicle to use in communicating general housekeeping updates. Taking the time to identify forms and frequency of communication in the beginning of a school year will assist you in establishing essential routines and procedures that can be counted on by staff members throughout the year. In planning for communication, you may wish to use a simple planning chart such as the one shown in Chart 4.1 to guide and focus your thinking.

Once you have established the general forms of communication you intend to use throughout the year, it is a good idea to actually schedule when they will be used. In other words, plan the dates for staff meetings, staff development sessions, bulletin dissemination, informal staff observations, and so on. Then, of course, communicate these dates to staff members.

Forms of Communication

A building leader will communicate with staff members in a variety of different ways. Analyzing each of these types of communication to clarify its purpose will assist a leader in planning and executing each form effectively. Once a purpose for a specified type of communication is identified the format, length, and frequency of use will become clear.

Staff Bulletins

Generating a weekly or bi-monthly staff bulletin is an efficient way to communicate general information to staff. If generated on a

Chart 4.1

Type	Purpose	Format	Frequency
Bulletin	Recognize achievements Share important dates Communicate district information	E-mail	Every other week Friday A.M.
Staff Meeting	Share data results Communicate expectations Gain feedback and ideas on initiatives	Face-to-face meeting	Bi-Monthly Wednesdays (8:05-8:55)
Staff Development Session	Instruct on new strategies Provide for team dialogue Share individual student data	Face-to-face meeting	Monthly Tuesdays (3:45-5:45)
Building Council Minutes	Share results from meeting discussion	Written memo	Monthly
Individual staff observation notes	Share observations from classroom visits and provide an opportunity for individuals to discuss practices/techniques	Short anecdotal notes	Bi-Monthly
Full School Assembly	Share school goals and achievements Communicate expectations	Schoolwide assembly with students	Once per semester

regular basis, staff will quickly learn to refer to this piece of communication for essential dates, upcoming activities, building news, and other pertinent information related to school or district business. In designing a staff bulletin, a leader may wish to keep two points in mind. First, the format and organization of the bulletin should be considered in relation to the audience it is directed toward. Second, the contents should be carefully planned and consistent in order to achieve maximum use by its intended audience.

As stated earlier, it is important that the communicator keep in mind the purpose of this type of communication and design the format to meet this intended purpose. Generally, staff bulletins are used to communicate important dates, upcoming events and activities, and established time lines or due dates, as well as providing staff members with pertinent district information such as upcoming coursework, district expectations, and changes in policies or procedures. In addition, a staff bulletin is also a nice vehicle in which to recognize staff accomplishments and praise personnel in print as a means of boosting morale and honoring the work and contributions of staff members.

Establishing a generic format for a staff bulletin will assist a leader in making sure that this document can be easily perused and efficiently used by staff members. The audience for the staff bulletin is obviously the staff; thus it makes sense to begin each bulletin with staff recognition. Starting each bulletin by noting specific staff contributions and offering thanks and praise for hard work will send a clear message that staff and their work are the driving force of the organization, and recognition in print serves as a powerful means for gaining the reader's attention.

A second section of a staff bulletin should clearly state upcoming events along with related dates, times, and staff expectations. This portion of the bulletin will be referred to the most by its readers and should be clearly written in a format that is organized and easily read. Bulleted lists of dates accompanied by short descriptions of events and activities or a table or chart of some type works well for highlighting this important information.

A section related to district news should also be included in staff bulletins. By providing staff members with regular updates regarding the happenings within the larger organization, staff can develop a sense of connectedness to the larger group. In addition, as building initiatives and events are planned and organized it is important for the leader to communicate how the site work is related to district plans and initiatives, as a means for cultivating a sense of continuity and clarifying for staff how their work at the site level fits in the larger organization.

As with any written communication, a leader needs to take care to ensure that his or her writing is not only clearly written, but also accurate in regard to grammar, punctuation, and spelling. With the technology currently available, there is truly no excuse for poorly written communication. If this is a challenge area for you, then it might be advantageous to ask a secretary or office staff member to edit your work prior to distributing it to the intended audience.

E-Mail Messages

In today's technological world, e-mail has become the most prevalent form of communication in all organizations. The school is no exception to this trend. In order for a leader to use e-mail communication effectively, he or she needs once again to consider the audience and the purpose of the communication.

E-mail is usually the most efficient means for quickly communicating urgent messages or information to all staff members. Leaders are best advised to set up group lists for disseminating e-mail memos to groups of individuals, which will expedite the process of getting information out quickly. Most school leaders find it helpful to set up the following groups within their e-mail lists:

Office Staff

Classroom Teachers

Grade-Level or Department Teams

Specialist Teams

Support Staff (Deans, Counselors, Advisors, etc.)

Certificated Staff

Classified Personnel

Committee Group Members

Once a leader has determined which groups he or she thinks would be useful, the task of setting up such groups can be delegated to an office staff member to complete.

E-mail messages are also a vehicle for reminding groups of individuals or the entire staff of due dates, special events, or routine activities. By planning in advance, most e-mail software can be programmed to automatically send out regular messages to groups. Thus, dates and groups designated to receive specific messages or reminders can be inputted at the beginning of a school year and/or on a semester or quarterly basis and then the computer is left to do the work while the leader moves on to other activities.

E-mail is also an efficient means for communicating with staff members to set up dates for meetings, observations, evaluation conferences, or other pertinent events. Most messaging systems are capable of checking individual calendars for available times, and if all parties use this feature, then important meetings or events can be scheduled quite quickly. If individuals do not keep their individual calendars up to date within the e-mail provider service, then setting up meetings can become a futile task laden with back-and-forth messages between both parties. If this is the scenario, it is simply more efficient to have a face-to-face dialogue where all parties have their individual calendar in hand.

Although it may be more efficient, e-mail can also be quite impersonal and if overused can leave staff feeling isolated and out of touch with their leader. These feelings are ones that a leader should avoid at all cost. Personal contact is a critical piece to maintaining a culture of open communication, and it allows for that human touch that most individuals thrive on.

Face-to-Face Interactive Communication

In addition to providing that human touch, face-to-face communication also allows for a deeper level of communication to occur because nonverbal messages come into the picture. Just like the phrase, "A picture is worth a thousand words," body behaviors send powerful nonverbal messages that can provide a great deal more information than the simple spoken words.

Face-to-face communication between a staff and a leader must be planned on a regular basis. Of course, individual communication occurs daily between individual staff members and a building leader, but there should also be opportunities at least every other week for the staff to gather in larger groups to communicate with the building leader. As with other types of communication discussed previously, these face-to-face interactions will be most effective if they are planned and are designed to meet the identified purpose.

Most often these larger group meetings are designed as a forum for sharing pertinent information in which feedback and input is necessary or to engage groups in learning situations. A leader needs to carefully weigh the items to be discussed in this type of forum and avoid having these sessions turn into an hour-long one-sided dialogue in which the leader simply shares announcements. Announcements and updates are best communicated in a written form such as a bulletin. If staff meetings turn into announcement meetings, over time staff members will begin to demonstrate annoyance, and rightly so, at their precious time being spent in this manner.

Nonverbal Communication

Nonverbal messages can serve as an additional source of information and when observed carefully will reveal hidden thoughts and messages that are not spoken. Too often these nonverbal cues go unnoticed, thus valuable pieces of communication are lost. Just as an experienced trainer or presenter learns the importance of reading his or her audience, a leader with strong communication skills learns how to analyze the meaning behind nonverbal cues and effectively communicate messages in a clear manner using body behavior as a vehicle for driving home an important point, putting a group at ease, or adding a needed tenor of authority.

There are several commonly used cues or behaviors that when analyzed communicate distinct messages. Tone of voice, body gestures including eye contact, and positioning in a room are some of the most prevalent nonverbal forms of communication. Once again, analyzing and understanding nonverbal messages can help individuals to better understand the communication they are receiving from others, and assist them in effectively communicating so that their messages are easily understood.

Raising and lowering one's voice is one technique often used to convey a specific message. A steady rise in one's voice leads a receiver to understand that the importance of an issue is climbing. In addition, lowering one's voice communicates honesty and empathy and is best used when communicating messages that may not be favorable or popular or when it is important for a group to learn that the leader is sharing his or her personal thoughts and feelings on a topic. A lowered voice also communicates a leader's feeling that his or her expectations have not been met, and receivers may feel as if they have been scolded if the content is related to performance, lowered data, or lack of achievement toward a set goal. The tone itself can send the message, even if the words are unclear.

Behavior analysts have found specific gestures to signal quite simplistic, nonverbal messages. Maintaining eye contact often communicates honesty, for example, while wandering or dodging eyes lead a receiver to believe that the communication is dishonest or incomplete. This same message of dishonesty is also communicated when individuals blink their eyes repeatedly or rub or touch their nose, which to the novice onlooker, may simply be viewed as someone adjusting a pair of glasses. When a leader avoids eye contact with those with whom he or she is communicating, and instead focuses his or her eyes on specific sheets of data or charts detailing specific information, the message received is that the speaker is not associated directly with the data and that he or she is not taking ownership for such results or outcomes. This technique may be wisely used by a new administrator highlighting low test data received by a school prior to his or her appointment as administrator.

Individuals who are uncomfortable or guarded may send out this message by body position and or the use of extremities. Individuals who sit with their arms crossed in front of their body, for example, are demonstrating a shield or barrier that communicates a strong differing opinion. A more blatant behavior is turning one's back to a speaker or communicator. This also sends a message that the individual is opposed to the message being communicated and is simply ignoring or disregarding it.

Recognizing these types of nonverbal messages is simply the first step in effective communication. The next step would be for a leader to specifically address the messages being sent in order to gain a clear understanding of what is being communicated. Leaders can address these issues in a nonthreatening manner, but making a simple statement such as, "I am sensing that some of you are not comfortable with the guidelines being discussed. Please share your specific reservations so we can approach them as a team and try and make everyone feel more at ease." If this open statement results in silence in the group, the leader may wish to play devil's advocate and take a stab at making a specific comment that he or she thinks may be making some in the group feel insecure or guarded. This may sound something like, "I would anticipate that some might be bothered by the increase in the number of formal observations being requested. I realize that observations mean additional meeting time for you both before and after the observation, and some of you may be wondering how you can fit everything into your already busy schedule." This type of comment will generally open the floodgate for comments. Make sure, if you use this tactic, that you are prepared to discuss your strategy for how their concerns can be alleviated. In some instances, you will not have the answers to their hard questions, but you can always open up the floor for suggestions on how to tackle the challenges so they don't become insurmountable obstacles.

Body position or grounding within a space also sends out nonverbal messages. A leader should identify various locations within a room to use as anchors for communicating various types of messages. For example, one anchor may be for relaxed messages or humor. Another location might be used when sending messages in which a sense of authority is desired. Finally, a leader should identify a location in a room to use when addressing adversarial messages from others. When the leader moves to these identified anchors within a room, receivers will attach their emotions to the locations rather than the individual communicating. The effect of not paying attention to this type of positioning could be receivers feeling that they can't take an individual seriously because they can't distinguish between when the person is joking versus when he or she is sending a serious message and using authority to share an expectation.

Genuine Listening

Listening skills are foundational to two-way communication. Genuine listening involves so much more than simply keeping one's ears open. An individual who genuinely listens clears his or her mind of personal thoughts in order to openly take in the full message being communicated. In addition, when an individual is truly listening, he or she does not question the communicator except when clarification is needed. This allows the message to be communicated as it was intended and allows the speaker to remain in control of the direction of the dialogue. This type of listening takes time and practice, and it sends out a definitive message that what the speaker has to say is viewed by the listener as important. If a leader wishes all staff members to develop the skills of genuine listening, then it is important that the leader openly share what genuine listening looks and sounds like. In addition, reiterating genuine listening behaviors on a regular basis will serve as a reminder of the expectations. Most important, the leader must commit him- or herself to modeling these behaviors for staff members.

Group Processing Strategies

In order for communication to occur in an effective manner and for two-way communication to be fostered within a large group, it is essential that a leader carefully consider various processes that can be used and select a method that will most efficiently move the group to reach the intended outcome. Below are just a few of the most common group processing strategies that can be used in face-to-face interaction that allow for input to be communicated, individuals' ideas to be shared and acknowledged, and goals or outcomes to be achieved efficiently.

Brainstorm, Classify, Label (BCL)

Using the BCL strategy, small groups begin by brainstorming ideas related to a given topic. (If sticky notes are used for the brainstorming, then the ideas can easily be manipulated in the next step of the process.) Once they have exhausted all possibilities for the brainstorming, the group members cluster the brainstormed ideas to form groups of ideas or thoughts that are related. Finally, each group of ideas is given a word or phrase as a label to identify the overall focus of the ideas. As category labels are shared with the large group, duplications are eliminated and similar labels are merged. The final outcome is that all ideas related to a topic or issue are shared and categorized so that everyone feels that their voice has been heard.

Jigsaw

The Jigsaw strategy is an effective means for groups to efficiently learn and share information. Groups are formed based on a specific task they are to complete or information they are to learn. For example, all members of group A may be asked to read the first chapter of a text, while group B reads Chapter 2, and so on. After each of the individuals has completed the assigned task, they come together to create an expert group. The experts on Chapter 1 will identify the key points from the reading as well as how to most effectively communicate what they have learned to others. Next, new groups are formed containing one individual from each of the previous expert groups. Once in this new group, members take turns sharing the highlights of the information from their assignment.

Gallery

Groups using the Gallery strategy brainstorm ideas on a specific topic and then design a chart, image, or written document that highlights the important findings and outcomes of the group on a large piece of chart paper. These posters of information are then posted around a room to create a gallery for groups to move through. Viewer response charts can be added alongside each of the pieces to provide a forum in which individuals or groups can respond to the information and/or record a question that they would like the original group to clarify.

Chapter Review

Of all the facets of leadership, effective communication to staff is probably the most powerful to building a strong foundation. Leaders communicate with staff members through writing, face-to-face verbal interaction, and nonverbal communication.

Careful planning and preparation is essential to all forms of communication. In the planning phase leaders must consider the audience, purpose, format, and frequency of communication. Outlining the types of communication to be used throughout a school year and scheduling these in advance will ensure that messages are given and received as intended.

Effective leaders communicate with staff members on a daily basis. A wide range of formats of written communication will be used to keep staff informed throughout the school year, with staff bulletins and e-mail messages being the most common. Face-to-face interactions require advance preparation in order to be effective, and the art of genuine listening is foundational to being able to receive and deliver messages clearly. Nonverbal messages are a powerful facet of communication that leaders must learn to access and read to ensure that messages are accurately interpreted and received as intended. Lastly, processes to engage staff members in discussions and to reach decisions in an efficient manner are critical to getting all staff members involved and committed.

Leaders who take the time to develop and practice the necessary skills of communication will find that they have the luxury of additional time—time that other leaders will be forced to spend rewriting unclear messages, backpedaling when they are blindsided by issues that have had time to fester as a result of their not being addressed head on, and fighting uphill battles to get individuals on board when their reservations communicated through nonverbal messages have been ignored.

Chapter 5

Communicating With Parents and Community Members

The same general rules of effective communication discussed in the previous chapter surrounding communicating with staff members also hold true for communicating effectively with parents and community members. Leaders need to practice their skills in genuine listening, use clear and straightforward written communication, and take the necessary time to plan and prepare for communication with these important individuals. Because the audience is different, there are some adjustments that need to be made when communicating with these individuals. In this chapter issues surrounding visibility, written communication, and face-to-face interactions with parents and community members will be addressed.

Visibility

As the old adage states, "Actions speak louder than words." Thus, visibility sends a critical message to parents and community members that is stronger than anything written or spoken. It is essential that leaders make themselves visible to these important stakeholders of a school community. When a leader is visible, parents and community members come to view the leader as someone who is actively involved in the everyday activities of a school. Strong visibility sends a clear message that the leader is guiding and supporting every aspect of the school vision in order to keep others focused and on track to reach identified goals. This leads to a sense of trust and security among parents and community members. In addition, parents are more inclined to develop a sense of comfort with a leader whom they see on a regular basis and will approach him or her in a calmer, more positive manner if they have issues or concerns to address.

Visibility means more than simply being outside or in common areas as students arrive and are dismissed from school. It means attending after school or evening functions where parents will be in attendance; being in classrooms, media centers, and hallways during the school day; dropping in on PTA sponsored events that occur at the school; attending sporting events or special club activities; and may even include hosting some informal parent-principal discussion sessions. Providing parents with office hours (days and times that you have designated in your weekly calendar to communicate with parents or community members) conveys that you are available for them and view interaction with them as a priority.

Being present at functions and within the school environment is one piece of the visibility puzzle. A second important element is taking the time to meet parents and community members and to provide a genuine welcome to them each and every time you encounter them. It takes only a minute to extend a hand and introduce yourself, but it goes a long way in making others feel comfortable and will send the message that you are not only happy they took the time to come up to the school, but also want them to come again. The entire building staff should make every effort to make individuals feel welcome within the school environment, and as a building leader, it is your responsibility to set this example and ensure that a positive atmosphere prevails throughout the building. Parents and community members who leave a school with a positive feeling will undoubtedly return. Return visits are crucial if an educational partnership between the home and the school is to be fostered.

Written Communication Basics

For the most part, the largest portion of a leader's communication with parents and community members will be through writing. Thus, the challenge is raised as to how to create written communication parents value enough to read. I believe the key here, again, lies with careful planning, which includes designing communication to suit the intended audience. Below are some basic essentials in effectively designing a written communication system for parents.

Regularity

Leaders must establish the frequency of different types of communication as well as identify when the communication will be dispersed. Monthly parent newsletters, for example, should always go out during the same week of each month. Parents will learn when to expect the newsletter and will be more prone to look for it if they can anticipate its arrival.

Simplicity

The language and style of a newsletter should be kept simple enough that a parent can quickly read through it to glean the essential information. If written communication is too lengthy, with a great deal of "extra" information added in, parents will tend to skim through the entire piece and may miss important information. This doesn't mean you need to avoid photos or graphics, but rather be selective as to what needs to be included in a document and what can be left out. This same guideline holds true for short pieces of communication, including letters of concern or alerts to parents. These types of communication should be short and to the point. There should be an emphasis on the facts and rationale behind decisions made or actions taken, followed by an outline of the next steps parents can expect. Including an array of details and elaborate descriptive language will only distract the readers and may lead them to draw inaccurate conclusions.

Leave Out the Jargon

Remember to consider the audience for whom a piece is being written and use appropriate language. Newsletters that are filled with educational jargon may lead to confusion and misinterpretation, and some may even find it offensive when important information is laden with terminology that is unfamiliar to the general public. Of course, there are times when it is important for parents and community members to learn critical educational terms, especially if they are words their children will be using. A simple glossary of essential terminology can easily be included in a newsletter to provide parents and community members with general understandings. If kept to a minimum, this type of feature can be a useful way to keep parents and community members properly informed as to what is occurring in education at the district, state, and possibly national level.

Format Consistency

Just as it was important to develop and use a consistent format for staff bulletins, it is also critical to abide by the same rule for regular forms of parent and community member communication. Monthly newsletters to the community, for example, should be developed using the same format each month. When the same format is used consistently, parents will learn just where to look for specific types of information and their cutting out certain sections for upcoming events will become routine. General categories for inclusion in a monthly newsletter to the community will be discussed in the next section, "Forms of Written Communication."

Forms of Written Communication

Generally, leaders have four primary purposes for designing written communication to parents and community members. The most common purpose is to share school information. This type of communication would include information related to school achievements, upcoming events, special dates to note, and, of course, the all-important school lunch menu at the elementary level. The second purpose for written communication from school to home and/or community is to alert parents to a specific situation involving the school. Generally, communication of this nature takes the form of a letter to the parents and other community members from the building leader and includes facts surrounding a specific situation and outlines actions taken. A third purpose for written communication is to request information from parents. Once again, this often takes the form of a letter from the building leader or a school-based leadership committee and often includes a piece to be completed by the receiver and returned to the school. School surveys would fall within this particular category. The last purpose is to express gratitude or to acknowledge an individual's or group's accomplishment. This may be in the form of an award or certificate, but most often simply takes the shape of a personal thank you note from the building leader. The most common form of written communication to address each of these purposes is described in greater detail below.

Parent/Community Member Newsletter

A regular parent/community member newsletter is an excellent vehicle for communicating general school information. This document should, of course, follow the guidelines identified previously and then should be designed to allow for readers to get the most out of it. Leaders may wish to consider the following categories to include in this type of communication:

Academic Accomplishments

When each issue starts with a review of academic accomplishments and highlights, readers are able to visibly see that student achievement is of utmost importance at the school. This section may include highlights related to recent performance assessments, in-building test data results, or simply specific strategies or academic focus points for the month. This category allows you as a building leader the opportunity to share with parents and community members what you are proud of and allows them to join in your celebrations. You also may wish to include at the conclusion of this section some ideas on how parents can support their children at home in refining and developing the skills and strategies being taught at school. These ideas for parents should be simple and realistic.

Calendar of Upcoming Events

Parents need to be informed of upcoming events and calendar adjustments. If you are interested in gaining greater attendance at school functions, the first step is to clearly advertise them in advance. A bulleted listing of important dates, including event or activity title and appropriate time, makes for easy reference for readers. For events that require elaboration, a detailed description can follow the calendar. A calendar may look something like the one depicted below:

March at a Glance

3	School Assembly, Weather Forecasting 1:00–2:00 p.m. (Gym)
17–18	Parent Teacher Conferences 3:30–6:00 p.m. (Classrooms)
20	Fifth-Grade Trip to Ocean, Journey 9:15–2:00 p.m.
23	Parent Teacher Association Meeting 7:00 p.m. (Room 5)
27	No School; Teacher Workday
30 – April 6	No School; Spring Recess

Parent Involvement

Parents often are unaware of all the different ways they can support the school. By including a section each month highlighting volunteer needs, you can give parents a better idea of just how they can be of assistance. This section should include suggestions with a variety of time spans in order to provide working parents or family members with viable options. Providing estimates related to the amount of time a particular activity or volunteer option will take ensures that readers will know in advance the boundaries of the commitment. Finally, make sure to include the name and phone number of the person readers may contact to get more information or to offer their assistance.

Student Highlights

Readers will be drawn to any publication that offers a section in which student work (writing samples, math explanations, artwork, etc.) is highlighted. This category may also include names of students to be recognized for special honors, awards, or certificates.

Grade-Level, Team, or Department News

Some leaders like to include a section in which teams report news and information pertinent to their particular level or discipline. This section might include descriptions of specific strategies being focused on within various content areas, upcoming deadlines for reports or large projects, and requests for classroom materials and supplies.

District News and Information

It is important that readers be informed about what is occurring at the district level as well as within their own community school. In this section, parents can learn about materials on display prior to adoptions, opportunities to serve on district-level committees, updates on district funding proposals, and any other pertinent information that may be of interest.

Community Resources/Events

Parents will appreciate information related to community resources that may be available or upcoming events. This section could include when Mobile Library Vans will be in the area, tutoring times and locations for SAT tests, dates for special speaking events that may be of interest to readers, and times for open skating at the local skating rink.

Letters

Throughout the school year there will be many times when a specific situation or event warrants a personal letter to parents or community members. Often this form of communication is used to reduce anxiety or clarify details, but personalized letters can also serve as a wonderful vehicle for sharing positive news regarding student achievement. Regardless of the identified purpose of the letter, leaders need to take care in planning and developing personal letters if they are to meet their purpose and ensure that the intended audience takes the time to read them.

When situations or events occur at school that have a potential impact on student safety, a personal letter is in order. Parents will appreciate knowing firsthand from a reliable source the details of what occurred, rather than hearing fragments from their children or neighbors who happened to be visiting the school. In addition, by designing and dispersing a personal letter on the day in which something has occurred, leaders can avoid the barrage of phone calls from concerned inquirers.

A letter may also be the best means for communicating pertinent information about any topic that is considered to be of high interest to parents and community members. Issues surrounding staffing changes for the following year, changes in school schedules, school-wide or district adoption of new materials, and final student achievement data are some examples for which a letter may be the most effective means of communication.

To be effective, leaders should follow some simple guidelines in designing personal letters to community members and parents. First, letters should be focused on a specific topic and should be kept brief and to the point. It is important that a leader state the facts surrounding the situation, the actions taken, and the final outcome. In some cases a rationale for actions taken may be appropriate. In many situations letters must be composed and distributed quickly, thus it is imperative to use concise language that communicates the essential information. And, as always, eliminate the educational jargon.

Special Announcements and Invitations

Flyers or invitations are another means of communication that may be used by a leader during a school year. Special events and or schoolwide activities should of course be discussed and advertised in a monthly newsletter, but in some instances a leader may wish to send out a special invitation or flyer to parents or community members as a reminder. These announcements can have a dramatic impact on the number of individuals who attend special school events.

Announcements or invitations should clearly state the title of the event along with a very brief description. In addition, the date, time, and location of the event should be visible as well as the cost for attendance, if appropriate. When these essential pieces of information are in a bulleted format, a reader will be able to quickly discern the intended information. Finally, in some cases it may be appropriate to list the benefits to those who attend. Copying flyers or announcements of this type on bright colored paper will also increase the odds of their being seen and read by the intended audience.

Face-to-Face Communication

Face-to-face communication between a school leader and parents or community members will look different based on the size and makeup of the group. It is hoped that leaders will address these important individuals informally on a daily basis. As parents or community members check in to volunteer in the building, seek out a guidance counselor for scheduling questions, stop in to pick up children, or to drop off a lunch that was left at home, a leader has a perfect opportunity for informal face-to-face communication. This type of informal communication is critical simply because it occurs so frequently. It is essential that a leader take the time to acknowledge a parent or community member and inquire as to whether or not he or she needs assistance. Offering a quick smile, a handshake, and a sincere thank you for support is a simple way to leave others with a positive impression.

Communication With Representative Committees

Leaders should also plan regular opportunities to meet face to face with groups of parents and community members. Most schools have active Parent Teacher Associations and Parent and Teacher Accountability Committees that come together on a regular basis for school-related business. Although these committees are usually made up of a small number of members, they provide a leader with an opportunity to communicate with a representative group that can provide valuable insights, opinions, and ideas shared by the larger population.

Face-to-face communication with representative groups such as those mentioned previously should be carefully planned in order to maximize effectiveness. A leader should take an active role in designing a reasonable agenda for these groups based on both the needs of the school and of the parent/community member group. Time schedules should be closely adhered to for these meetings in order to honor everyone's time. Generally, PTA meetings are scheduled for an hour, once per month, and Accountability Committees meet for 1½ hours, eight or nine times throughout the school year. Providing light refreshments at these gatherings will set a positive and welcome atmosphere that will be greatly appreciated by all those attending. Finally, including a limited amount of time in the agenda for questions and for members to bring up additional issues and concerns for discussion will ensure that members feel that their input and concerns are welcome.

During meetings it is the leader's responsibility to model effective communication skills by using genuine listening techniques and embedding opportunities for members to effectively interact with one another as issues are addressed. The same types of communication processes discussed in the previous chapter for communicating with staff members can also be used with these groups. In addition, leaders should make sure to keep these groups updated as to actions that have taken place since the last meeting and how those actions reflect the recommendations of the group. Taking time to update members keeps them aware of new developments and also allows them to see that their work within the group is valued and their ideas and opinions have been heard.

Some leaders find it helpful to place upcoming meeting times and agendas in a monthly parent/community member newsletter. This technique may be helpful in encouraging nonmembers to attend the meeting and will send the message that everyone is welcome. All regular members should be provided with a meeting reminder note and an agenda one week prior to the scheduled meeting time.

Large Group Communication

It is essential that a leader plan time throughout the school year during which face-to-face communication with the entire parent and community group can occur. Back-to-school nights, parent information nights, and end-of-year recognition and award ceremonies lend themselves to this type of formal communication. These large group meetings provide a leader with an opportunity to share essential information with parents, and the information should be focused on critical issues about which all would be concerned. Below is a listing of some of the most common topics addressed at these large group meetings:

School academic status

School values and vision statement

Goals and progress updates

Discipline policy

General budget information

Special school-based programs, clubs, sports

Volunteer opportunities

Descriptions of working committees in need of members

Meetings that involve the total parent and community member group should be kept brief and informative. In planning these types of sessions, the leader must pay close attention to the audience and design the presentation accordingly. Visuals such as charts and graphs to share student achievement data are effective tools if they are kept simple and can be easily seen by a large audience (overheads or LCD screens serve this purpose well). Eliminating educational jargon will be greatly appreciated by a parent audience and will ensure that messages are clear and understood by everyone. Providing attendees with a written document that highlights the critical topics addressed allows the audience to leave with the information in hand for future reference.

Chapter Review

A leader must develop the skills necessary to effectively communicate with parents and community members. At the most foundational level is the informal communication that occurs as a result of a leader's being visible at a school site. This informal communication sends out a very powerful message related to a leader's involvement in all activities within a school. A leader can make parents and community members feel welcome simply by acknowledging their presence and taking a moment to say hello.

Leaders will communicate with parents and community members most often through writing, thus it is imperative that they carefully plan their written communication in order to effectively address the intended audience. Ensuring that the format closely matches the purpose of the communication is key to making written communication easy to read and understand. In addition, a leader will find that using a consistent format and releasing regular communication pieces on a consistent schedule will increase the percentage of receivers who will take the time to read the communication.

Face-to-face communication with parents and community members should be planned and scheduled to occur throughout the school year. Both small group meetings and large group informational sessions are necessary to effectively communicate important information to parents and community members. Small group meetings should provide opportunities for members to interact and share their ideas and thoughts surrounding critical issues related to the school. Large group meetings should be kept brief and generally will focus on topics that are pertinent to all members of the audience. The key to all types of communication is careful planning and consideration of the audience being addressed.

Chapter 6

Communicating With District Personnel

Regardless of the size of a district, a school leader will always have district personnel with whom he or she must communicate. In smaller districts, a building leader may communicate only with a district superintendent and possibly a director of facilities. In larger organizations, a leader may communicate with district personnel from more than 20 different departments. Although smaller districts may have a less formalized system for communicating with building leaders, the foundational skills a leader will need to exercise in communicating with district personnel will be fairly consistent from small organizations to larger ones. In communicating with district personnel, leaders will need skills in listening, oral and written discourse, and interpreting and using nonverbal communication. Sound familiar? These essential skills of communication remain the same regardless of the audience. There are some unique considerations that administrators should take note of when communicating with district personnel. These issues are addressed in this chapter under the following headings:

Considering the District Viewpoint

Communicating Building Needs

Managing the District Paper Trail

Sharing Building Information

Considering the District Viewpoint

There are some important details to keep in mind when communicating with district personnel. First, district personnel view the building administrator and each individual school site as one piece of a larger, much more intricate puzzle. Thus, when communicating with district personnel it is imperative to keep this view in mind. This view will drive the amount and type of information communicated. Communication to district personnel should generally be kept brief; remember you are only one of many communicating with the same group of individuals. In addition, district personnel will filter information through a lens that requires them to ask how the information will impact the district as a whole.

If you are proposing a change in bus schedule for your school site, for example, district personnel will consider not only the benefits for your school but also the potential ramifications for the entire system. The wise administrator will think through this lens him- or herself prior to beginning any type of communication with district personnel so that potential obstacles can be considered and possible solutions thought out. Then, when planning the communication, the administrator can disclose potential problems along with possible solutions. Obstacles never seem as insurmountable when they are offered up openly along with some viable solutions for overcoming them.

Glancing through this district lens from time to time will assist administrators in keeping a larger perspective than that experienced at their site on a daily basis. With this perspective in mind, communicating building events to district personnel may assist a building administrator to avoid conflicts with neighboring schools or community events. Often district personnel maintain a large events calendar that they use in scheduling districtwide functions. By communicating the dates, times, and details of events scheduled to occur at your individual site, you can ensure that they are included in the larger calendar, thus reducing the risk of multiple events competing for parents' or community members' attention. This information can easily be sent to the district office on a monthly basis and should be written in a simple-to-read calendar format such as "March at a Glance" in Chapter 5, used for sharing key dates and events in the Parent/Community Newsletters.

A second important point to remember is that district personnel are interested in how a school site is functioning in regard to district-wide initiatives. When communicating to these individuals about building programs, assessment data, or community activities, it is imperative that an administrator share how the site information being presented fits with respect to the larger district plan. Prefacing information being communicated with a simple statement about how the data or information being shared relates to a particular district focus or initiative will make sure that everyone is clear on where the information fits within the larger picture. A statement such as the one given below is sufficient to meet this purpose:

District Initiative: Increase student achievement in reading and writing

Descriptive statement to accompany data: In our efforts to increase student achievement in writing, Century has been gathering and compiling data on student performance in each of the stages of the writing process on a quarterly basis. Attached is a chart depicting our results for the fourth quarter.

Communicating Building Needs

Once again, consideration of the audience is a crucial piece in planning and delivering communication to district personnel. There will be an abundance of both written and verbal communication that will go back and forth between a building administrator and the many members making up the district personnel team. In planning communication of building needs to these individuals it is important to keep the following two guidelines in mind:

State the facts: District personnel do not have time for a lot of scrupulous details and flowery language; remember you are one of many to whom they must respond and communicate on a regular basis. They are interested in knowing simply what occurred, what action was taken, and what the next steps are. Your personal opinions and any type of inflammatory language can only come back to haunt you, so it is best to leave it out.

Make requests rather than demands: Making demands of district personnel generally does not go over well. Requesting their assistance is a different story. When you do wish for more help than simple advice, putting your request in writing is good practice. For example, if you have a group of parents up in arms about a new district policy, and even after you have done your best to address their concerns and calm them down they are still upset, you may wish to request a district spokesperson come in and address the group in an open forum. In formulating this type of request in writing you would want to describe the situation, explain what you have done to resolve the issue, clearly state what you are requesting in the form of district support, and what outcome you hope to achieve as a result of the request. If you have a particular individual in mind for filling the request, you also may wish to make a recommendation and state your reasons why you feel that individual would best meet your school's needs. Regardless of the request, make every effort to give the district adequate time to fill it.

In a crisis situation, of course, these rules simply do not apply. Some situations warrant making demands, and any situation in which your students, staff, or the community at large is in danger is reason enough for you to speak up and tell the district what you need and when. As the building administrator it is your call as to whether or not the situation you are facing requires this type of immediate support. My advice is to always lean toward being cautious. Don't second-guess yourself; when in doubt, call in the reinforcements. No one will ever condemn you for being too careful when it comes to protecting your students, staff, and community. And, never underestimate what the district forces are able to accomplish when one of their own is in need. I have always been amazed by the talent, expertise, and devotion that surface when a crisis arises.

Thank goodness, the crisis situations are few and far between for a building administrator. On the other hand, there will be many occasions when situations arise in which it is wise to gain the expertise and advice of an individual from the district office before taking action yourself. Some may view this as weakness, or an inability to act independently, but I see it as being careful and making intelligent use of all your resources. You cannot assume that district personnel can simply leave their daily duties to come to your assistance each and every time you hit a bump in the administrative path, but my experience has shown that there is always someone willing to lend an ear and offer a piece of helpful advice. In a large organization, it is sometimes a challenge to find just who to contact for this type of support, but believe me, the other building administrators, your peers, know who to turn to, so simply ask them for guidance.

Managing the District Paper Trail

One of the duties assigned to a building administrator is completing all the various forms and documents associated with the general management of a school building. The format of this type of managerial written communication is often determined by the district and distributed to administrators in the form of information tables, worksheets, or action plan documents to be completed with pertinent site information. In addition, the district often dictates the time lines for completion of districtwide forms and plans. For example, building budgets are generally completed using a district template and are due at the district budget office by a designated date. There is an abundance of this formal type of written communication in which a district dictates to a building administrator the information to be communicated, in what format, and the deadline for completion. When communicating information using these types of documents, an administrator will be appreciated for carefully completing all portions of a form correctly, checking work to make sure that data make sense and are accurate (especially important when reporting data in which numbers have to add up), and submitting the form by the designated due date. For larger projects, it may be helpful to design a plan for completing a long-range project, as discussed in the Organization section of this book. There will be at least one individual at the district office who will be assigned the arduous task of cumulating information from all building administrators, and you can imagine how frustrating it is if forms are not turned in on time, or information is inaccurate or missing. Just think of how you feel when your staff is given a task to complete and you as the building administrator have to track individuals down to get late forms, or to clarify information that was not accurate in the original document submitted.

Keeping abreast of these managerial tasks is crucial if one is to survive as a building administrator. John Daresh makes this point quite well when, in his text *Beginning the Principalship,* he writes, "A person can never serve as a true leader if he or she does not also survive as a manager. The job has to be done." Many reports and pieces of data are requested on a yearly basis, thus an administrator can plan ahead and complete them in advance. Most administrators find it helpful to maintain an updated list of reports and documents that are due at the district each fall and spring as a beginning point. These annual pieces of communication may not change significantly from one year to the next, and in many cases a building secretary can update information and send it on to the district office if an administrator alerts him or her to critical due dates.

Throughout the school year district personnel will also assign new tasks to building administrators. By following the guidelines outlined in Section I of this text, administrators will be able to plan effectively for the completion of both short- and long-term projects in order to ensure that information is submitted in a timely manner. A simple strategy is to schedule and block out a piece of time each week to complete district paperwork.

Most organizations today use an intranet service through which a great deal of communication occurs between a building administrator and district personnel. Once again, the key to managing e-mail efficiently is keeping up with it on a regular basis. Scheduling time to review and respond to e-mail on a daily basis is a necessity in today's technological society. If e-mail is left unattended for several days, the task of reading through it all and responding to critical pieces can soak up a large chunk of valuable time. By keeping up with tasks on a regular basis, the paper trail will not become an overwhelming beast.

Sharing Building Information

What do you wish the district office to know about your school? This is a key question to consider when determining what pieces of information to share with district personnel. District personnel will always be privy to the details regarding what parents or staff are unhappy about; yes, it is true that bad news travels fast. But generally they will hear the good news only if an administrator takes the time to communicate it to them. In order to gain a clear picture of what is actually occurring at an individual school site, district personnel must depend on the communication they receive from building leaders. Building leaders should communicate school information in writing as well as in person through face-to-face interaction.

Written Communication

There are a few critical pieces of written communication that should be provided to district personnel on a regular basis. First, someone in the administrative offices should receive a copy of the monthly newsletter that is sent out to the parents and community members of the school. At the beginning of the school year, compile a list of individuals for your secretary to send newsletters to on a monthly basis and then leave it up to him or her to complete the task. Key individuals to send these newsletters to include the following:

Board Member(s)

Director of District Communication and/or Public Relations Director

Immediate Supervisor

In addition to the monthly newsletter, a monthly calendar of events for the school should also be sent on a regular basis to the above individuals. The third piece of written communication that should be sent to district personnel on a regular basis is school-based student achievement results. In most instances, school sites collect and tabulate student achievement data on a monthly, quarterly, or at minimum a semester basis. A copy of these results should always be communicated to district personnel. Achievement results should be sent to the individuals mentioned above, as well as to district-level curriculum and instruction personnel. Sharing these data sends a very clear message that at your school data are important and are regularly used to measure student achievement. It also will give district personnel a reason to celebrate with you and your staff when gains are made. Staff members will truly appreciate recognition of their accomplishments that often come as a result of sharing achievement data with district personnel.

E-mail can be a valuable resource for a busy administrator to keep communication lines open with district personnel. E-mail messages can easily be sent as a follow up to critical in-person or phone communications, and when used in this manner they provide written documentation as to what was verbally agreed upon and can be used to outline, in writing, next steps of action. Also, many administrators make use of e-mail for communicating school events and building news to district personnel. As discussed earlier, e-mail is an informal, less personal form of communication and is not appropriate for all messages.

Face-to-Face Communication

Some pertinent building information should be communicated to district personnel in a more personalized manner. This generally will take the shape of a formal meeting during which time a building leader can communicate with district personnel face to face. There are two general categories in which a face-to-face meeting is the most appropriate form of communication. The first deals with building action plans and goals, and the second centers around issues in which confidentiality is of importance.

In order for district personnel to truly gain a sense of a building's goals and action plans, face-to-face communication is critical. These meetings will be most effective if they are carefully planned by the administrator and/or a building leadership team. The communication should include, first, a brief overview of the school's mission or the underlying values that run the organization, followed by how this information relates to the overall mission of the school district. Next, a leader should proceed to share the goals that have been set by the school in an effort to accomplish the mission or uphold the established values. Then, information related to the goals should be shared. This would include a dialogue regarding pre-assessment information, types of assessment tools to be used, and time lines for data collection. Last, the administrator should include how these data will be used to drive instructional practice within the building. This type of meeting should always end with a note on how data will be shared with staff, students, parents, and district personnel. Follow-up meetings related to building goals and data would be more focused on the results of data compiled and the next steps for students and staff based on the results.

Face-to-face communication allows a building administrator to truly share his or her enthusiasm for what is happening at a school. When the meeting is hosted at the school site, district personnel can have the opportunity to visit classrooms and gain a realistic sense of what is occurring throughout the school in relation to the values and goals. This type of information simply can't be sent in a written memo.

Communicating delicate issues in which confidentiality is of great importance also demands face-to-face communication with district personnel. Although these meetings often will end with the development of a written summary, it is usually helpful to begin with a verbal, more personalized discussion. One reason to meet with district personnel in person when these delicate types of issues arise is to provide an opportunity for everyone to review written data and documentation that have been compiled. School-district attorneys, personnel directors, and union representatives may be intimidating to a newer administrator, but it is important for a leader to remember that all of these individuals make up a large network of support within the district, and they are there to offer their expertise and services to building administrators and district employees in general.

These types of meetings also require careful planning on the part of the administrator. Regardless of the situation, it is imperative that facts surrounding the situation be documented so they can be easily communicated. It is also helpful to place events in sequential order with accurate dates and times, when known. The administrator should also make sure to have ready and available all critical records and any paperwork that may be requested for review by those attending the meeting. When verbally communicating to others in this type of situation, the leader should be careful to state the facts surrounding the situation and disclose any actions taken by school personnel or the administrator him- or herself. At the conclusion of the meeting it should be determined who will be responsible for creating a written summary of what was discussed as well as an outline of agreements made or next steps to be taken.

Chapter Review

As building administrators communicate with key district personnel it is imperative for them to keep in mind that they and their school site are simply one entity in a larger organization. District personnel will always be looking through this larger lens as communication is shared and received, thus it is imperative that an administrator consider this perspective as when planning communication with district personnel. Making sure to share with district personnel exactly how school events and goals fit beneath the umbrella that makes up the district's initiatives or outcomes is one way to ensure that information is filtered and received accurately.

When communicating information to district personnel, building administrators should follow the guidelines of sticking to the facts and making requests rather than demands. Avoid descriptive details when they are not needed to make communication clear and more productive. District personnel can be of great support to a building administrator and should be viewed as an extensive system of additional resources, but it is not appropriate to demand their services. District personnel can be of vital importance to making a school site run efficiently and effectively, and maintaining open and productive communication with these individuals will yield enormous benefits.

Keeping up with the paper trail can become quite a challenge, especially for a new administrator. Advance planning and scheduling regular work time to complete district tasks is one way to ensure that projects are completed accurately and in a timely manner. Attending to the details of tasks assigned by district personnel will be greatly appreciated, as will submitting work by the assigned due dates.

Last, there are critical pieces of communication that should be shared with district personnel throughout a school year. Keeping district members up to date on school events and activities as well as buildingwide data results should be a top priority for building administrators. Some pieces of communication are most appropriately shared through regular face-to-face communication with district personnel. Face-to-face communication is the most effective means for communicating information related to building action plans and goals, as well as discussions related to highly confidential situations.

Section III

Empowerment

As accountability for student achievement has risen over the course of the past decade, the role of the school administrator has significantly changed. In our current educational arena, the principal is responsible not only for performing the duties necessary to effectively manage a school site, but more important, for serving as an educational leader who can support and coach teachers in the implementation of research-based practices designed to improve student achievement in order to meet state and district standards. This shift in the leadership role has dramatically raised the bar in regard to what defines an effective administrator. Administrators are finding themselves pulled and stretched in many different directions, and for many, this new role as an educational leader appears to be an unreachable goal. Even the most energetic and enthusiastic novices in the profession soon realize that blood, sweat, and tears alone are simply not enough to move them to the high level of success they aspire to achieve. The key to achieving and maintaining such success lies with a leader's ability to effectively empower others.

States will continue to establish standards, districts will follow suit and design their own achievement initiatives to meet the state standards, and building leaders will develop their own individual visions for their sites in relation to how to raise student achievement to the identified levels, but without the committed efforts of all staff members the initiatives and visions will be left on chart paper and forgotten when classroom doors close. Through empowerment, leaders have the ability to work with their staff in an effort to clarify values and goals and to establish commitment statements that staff have not only designed and agreed upon, but for which they are willing to be held accountable. When a staff joins together and commits to initiatives, they become armed with the power to make systemic change that will have a positive and dramatic effect on student achievement.

In nature, the concept of empowerment can be viewed in the behavior of geese. Geese fly in a "V" formation for reasons beyond creating a beautiful image for humans to observe in the sky. The "V" formation allows geese to use one another's strength to move at a quicker speed. By working together toward a common goal, they are rewarded by experiencing a dramatic uplift. They expend less energy and can move faster when they work collaboratively. In addition, geese alternate positions within the formation, taking turns leading the way. In other words, they are willing to be led by one another and also to take their turn serving as the pace setter and leader. Next, geese are compassionate and supportive of each other. When one of the flock becomes injured, one or two of their comrades leave the formation along with the injured or ill goose and tend to it until it either regains its strength and can return to the group or dies. Staff members will go through ups and downs. From time to time they too will require and deserve the support of their peers. Finally, geese honk at each other throughout their flight. Honking can be related to our form of cheering. Geese encourage one another to keep moving in their determined direction in order to meet their collective goal. Without honking, or encouragement, a staff can easily become discouraged when obstacles block their path. Then, instead of working together and harnessing their collective energy and creativity, which is necessary to move forward, they find themselves blocked by obstacles and they either lose sight of their goals, or worse, see their goals as unattainable. Unfortunately, the old adage, "Misery loves company," holds true within this scenario. If, when one goose begins to lose sight of goals and falls from the formation, others aren't around to encourage it and bring it back into the flock, it can have the power to bring others down with it. Before long, the entire flock can lose sight of where they are heading and the momentum can be completely lost. But the day can be saved if the courageous and ever-positive educational leader steps in to remind the flock of where they are heading and why they are heading there and offer encouragement so staff members can see that together they do have the power to meet any challenge.

Thus, the educational leader must develop the skills and strategies necessary to empower staff members and also be able to step in to serve as their leader to remind them of their goals, hold them accountable for their commitments, and energize them to continue their quest. The staff members of Century Elementary taught me many valuable lessons related to empowerment that will be shared in the next three chapters of this text. The first of these three chapters deals with a fundamental concept related to empowerment: the issue of losing control versus providing support. This will be followed by a discussion surrounding the development and incorporation of leadership teams. The final chapter in this section will focus on the use of data as a means of gaining staff commitment and empowering individuals to become individually accountable for the achievement of a site's goals and values.

Chapter 7

Giving Up Control and Extending Support

Empowerment means that a leader must be willing to give up some control and then have the skill and knowledge necessary to support others in order to ensure success. Trust, planning, and communication are the key ingredients in creating an environment in which individuals feel empowered, take on leadership roles with energy and enthusiasm, and achieve high levels of success in completing their identified outcomes and goals.

Trust

Giving up control requires trust. Trust is fostered when individuals and groups are given an opportunity to demonstrate their capabilities and complete tasks successfully. Thus, leaders are faced with a "Catch 22" situation. If they are not willing to trust, others will not have the opportunity to demonstrate their trustworthiness. As a result, empowerment requires a leader to initially extend trust to others based on little more than faith. A leader's willingness to extend trust to the staff with whom he or she works may not be enough. Trust, like effective communication, is a two-way street. Individuals must be willing to take on the challenge presented by empowerment, and in most situations they will take this step only if they trust the individual in the position to empower, namely the leader. Leaders earn trust by saying what they mean, meaning what they say, and following through on their commitments. It also doesn't hurt to demonstrate humanness by admitting when you are wrong or simply don't know something. Many training books include activities designed to enhance trust within the work place. See the Resources section of this text for a list of titles.

Planning and Communicating

A leader must feel confident that when he or she empowers others tasks will be completed in a timely manner and at an acceptable level of proficiency. So, for those lacking in the faith department, leaders can ensure success by instituting a critical safety net for individuals they empower. This safety net consists of careful planning and communication. Prior to empowering others, leaders must begin the planning process by first establishing bottom-line expectations for staff members. Then, to bring everyone on board, a leader must clearly communicate these expectations to the staff. Staff cannot be expected to adhere to guidelines that they do not know exist. Often these expectations are dictated by districts or states in the form of standards or descriptions of best practices. In regard to writing, for example, leaders may set forth an expectation that on a daily basis writing be modeled by teachers, and students be engaged in writing that involves the various stages of the writing process. Once this expectation is formulated and communicated, staff members are empowered to use their own creativity and knowledge base to design lesson plans to meet the needs of students in their own classrooms, while still ensuring that the bottom-line expectations set forth by the leader are honored. If a leader wants staff members to take ownership for the expectations, he or she can stretch empowerment a bit further by involving staff members during the planning stage. Representative members can be asked to serve on a committee to review standards and work collaboratively to design schoolwide expectations in order to meet the identified standards, thus giving the staff greater ownership of the expectations themselves. Additional information related to the formulation of leadership teams follows in Chapter 8.

Also in the planning phase, a leader should formulate a variety of processes that could effectively be used by staff members to meet expectations or complete tasks. It is helpful to identify for staff current practices that are already in place that could be used to meet new expectations. In reference to the writing expectation stated above, staff members who already have a writer's workshop approach in place in their classrooms, would benefit from knowing how this approach can be used to meet the stated expectation of teachers modeling writing and children writing themselves on a daily basis. Finding a link between current practice and proposed techniques or processes is another critical element to successfully gaining staff commitment to new initiatives and expectations.

If a leader is empowering a small group of individuals to complete a specified task it is imperative that he or she carefully communicate desired outcomes and facilitate and explain processes to assist teams in reaching their goal(s). The following checklist may serve as a guide for leaders in regard to offering support to teams as leaders begin to relinquish their own control and empower others to complete specified tasks.

- Clearly state the intended outcome, goal, or expectation.
- Identify reasonable time lines (including dates for smaller tasks related to the goal).
- Investigate and secure necessary resources (funding for paying individuals or groups to work beyond their duty day and/or to release them from their regular duties within the work day, determine who will support the team in regard to typing documents, etc.).
- Outline a process for individuals and/or groups to use in achieving the goal (the leader must realize that individuals or teams may choose to accomplish the task in a different manner, and he or she must be willing to allow for this flexibility).
- Schedule work time for groups (this may involve grade-level or cross grade-level planning time or time for small committees representing large groups to meet).

- Schedule time for individuals and/or teams to debrief and share outcome(s) with those whom they represent (this could take place at smaller team or department meetings or at a full staff meeting).
- Schedule time to meet on a regular basis with those empowered to debrief progress and assist in overcoming obstacles (this needs to occur only if the leader is not directly involved in a particular task assigned).

Support

Support comes in many shapes and sizes. Support means being clear in the beginning and sticking to original outcomes so individuals' time is not wasted. It means being there as an administrator to offer advice when difficult challenges come up. In addition, support also means standing behind the work created by staff members and giving them credit for their work. Finally, support means honoring the dedication and diligence of staff members by commending them for a job well done and by providing time for teams to share their accomplishments with the rest of the staff. When a staff feels the support of the administrator, they will be willing to go the extra mile and put forth energy to take on new and worthwhile challenges because they know that there is someone behind them to catch them if they fall and to offer additional help when the battle appears to be all uphill. In the end, when tasks are completed successfully everyone wins; leaders have a greater sense of trust for staff members, staff members know that they can rely upon and trust their leader, staff have a higher level of ownership of the work completed and are more willing to move forward with recommendations and projects, important tasks get completed in a timely manner, and in most cases the leader is given the precious gift of time to dedicate to other projects.

Chapter Review

Empowering others can be a scary proposition because it involves a high level of trust. Leaders must learn to trust others as well as gain the trust of those with whom they work as the first step. In addition, leaders also need to develop the necessary planning skills if empowerment is to be successful. Leaders who take the time to plan carefully will be rewarded with staff members who can reach goals and complete assigned tasks successfully.

There are many benefits to empowering staff members. Increased ownership and accountability is one of the most profound benefits that results from empowerment. If executed carefully, empowerment can also provide a leader with additional time. When a leader uses careful planning techniques, individuals and teams are often able to complete identified tasks independently without the direct supervision of the leader. Thus, important tasks and projects get completed while the leader dedicates his or her time to a wide range of other duties.

Empowerment requires leaders to give up some of their own control and at the same time extend necessary support. For some administrators, relinquishing control is without question the most difficult part because it requires a shift in paradigm. The traditional administrator role put a leader in the position of always being in control, but as the administrator role shifted to encompass a greater span of duties, the necessity for empowerment of others emerged. In today's educational arena empowerment is a key to survival for administrators. The ability to extend support to those empowered is a crucial element, and support can take on many different shapes and sizes depending on the dynamics of the group and the task or project assigned.

Chapter 8

Designing and Implementing Leadership Teams

Developing and implementing leadership teams at an individual school site or within a department can offer a leader an enormous amount of support. In addition, leadership teams are a natural vehicle for empowering others, which will increase individual and group ownership and ultimately accountability for results. In his powerful text, *Leading in a Culture of Change,* Fullan writes, "Principals and teachers will only be mobilized by caring and respect, by talented people working together, and by developing shared expertise." This chapter focuses on the steps related to the development and implementation of leadership teams, which is one way to begin

Fullan's vision. Discussions surrounding the identification of leadership team outcomes, group size, team makeup, and tips for successful meetings are included.

Identifying Team Outcomes

Once it has been determined that the formation of a leadership team would be beneficial to a site or department, it is critical that the outcomes for the group be carefully designed. The entire staff should be involved in outlining the tasks and responsibilities of the leadership team. The leader will be instrumental in guiding this discussion to ensure that the identified outcomes are in line with the building and district expectations and needs. It will become the leader's responsibility to oversee the leadership team's work and to be ultimately accountable for achieving intended results. The two most common outcomes addressed by leadership teams are (a) reviewing and analyzing assessment data, and (b) designing a time line and schedule for professional development for a site that is differentiated and based on needs as derived from data analysis. Outcomes will vary from site to site, and it is critical that the staff members have some ownership of the work that this group will accomplish.

The process of identifying outcomes for a leadership team can begin with a simple brainstorming of possibilities. It is important that all staff members to take part in this initial stage of outcome development to ensure full staff support for the team's later work. The leader should also take an active role along with the staff during the brainstorming process to ensure that important tasks such as analyzing site data and determining and planning professional development needs be included as possible team outcomes. Regardless of the size of the staff, brainstorming will be most effective in small groups (6-10 people) in which a facilitator and a recorder have been assigned. Groups should have an opportunity to share their ideas, and this can be done quite efficiently even if with a large staff if a systematic process for sharing is used. An effective technique is to have the recorders stand alongside their brainstorming chart with a marker in hand. Each group shares one to three ideas from their chart. As ideas are given, recorders check off similar thoughts on their charts. As the recorders share, they report only new ideas from their group's chart. The sharing continues until all new ideas have been shared. A group recorder can list ideas shared on one large chart paper to serve as a full staff brainstorm list. Once potential outcomes have been identified, a small representative group can move through a process to prioritize outcomes. Leaders may wish to involve this group in a process of organizing the brainstormed items into categories such as those suggested for prioritizing tasks in Section I of this text ("Must Do," "Should Do" and "Would Be Nice"). Once categorized, the list of items in the "Must Do" section should be analyzed more closely in an effort to determine the top priority items to be covered initially by the leadership team. Often the amount of items in the "Must Do" category is sufficient to fill the time the leadership team will meet for the year. If not, the second priority category, "Should Do," can be reviewed and analyzed for additional outcomes.

Forming a Leadership Team

Once the outcomes for the leadership team have been clearly stated, the next step is to secure membership. It is imperative that the leader carefully consider the makeup of leadership teams in order to ensure their success. Group size, cross representation from the larger organization, and the ability level, talents, and experience of members all need to be taken into consideration prior to forming a leadership team.

Group Size. The most successful teams have enough members to allow for verbal engagement and dialogue, but not so many as to allow for some members to slip off into the scenery and not participate. The group should be able to successfully collaborate as a team without needing to subdivide to complete a task. Generally, teams of six to nine work best, but of course there are always other factors that may impact the actual size of a group. Secondary schools that employ 80 staff members would need a larger number of leadership team members in order to ensure adequate representation. I would highly encourage leaders to keep the membership number to 15 or less.

Group Member Makeup

It is critical that there is representation from all aspects of a staff or department on the leadership team. For every site this means something different, but in most cases it is important to have a member representing

- All types of staff members (classified as well as certificated),
- All levels (primary and intermediate or grade-level teams),

- All departments (special education, specialists, disciplines at the high school level, etc.), and
- All levels of experience (experienced personnel as well as those new to the profession).

Finally, it is important to consider the talents and knowledge base of the group members and ensure that there is a range of expertise among them in various areas. This will make for a more well-rounded group that can effectively tackle a wide range of tasks.

In a perfect world, a leader would simply ask for volunteers to join a leadership team and miraculously the members would step forward to create a group that truly represents all aspects of the organization and will effectively serve the purpose intended for the group. Unfortunately, this is not realistic. Of course, asking for volunteers may be a good first step, but a leader must be prepared to personally invite individuals to serve on the leadership team in order to ensure cross representation, balance, and the formation of a group that can achieve the intended outcomes identified earlier.

Steps to Ensure Team Success

Once the group members have been identified the leader will need to take steps to ensure their success by first clarifying the team's outcomes based upon the prioritized list. Team outcomes should be written in clear terms and should include information regarding how the success of team outcomes will be assessed and evaluated and specific time frames for accomplishing goals and objectives. After team outcomes, assessment information, and time lines are established, they should be communicated to the entire staff. Keeping all staff members informed is critical if staff members are going to take ownership and commit to being held accountable for the work generated by the leadership team.

A second step a leader will need to take to ensure the success of the leadership team is to schedule team meeting times for the year or at least for a semester. Meetings should be scheduled to occur on a regular basis throughout the school year, and identified dates and times should be added to the school calendar to avoid conflicts later. In most schools, leadership teams meet at least monthly. In addition, the leader may wish to assign a chairperson to serve as the team's leader, or the team itself can meet to discuss who might be willing and able to serve in this capacity. The chairperson will be in charge of working closely with the administrator to finalize agendas and formulate appropriate processes to use with the group as well as keeping the group on task and focused during meetings.

Planning is essential if leadership team meetings are to run smoothly so that identified results can be efficiently achieved. Establishing short-term, realistic goals is one way to keep a team on target. Accomplishment of smaller goals will also build morale among members and provide opportunities for celebration, which will breathe new energy into a group. Even the most challenging of goals can be accomplished if broken down into manageable pieces. By working collaboratively with the leadership team chairperson, a leader can design a framework for the team to work from in accomplishing complicated goals. This framework should include details regarding what a task will look like when complete, as well as realistic time frames for task completion. It is through organized planning that larger tasks will be successfully accomplished. Sometimes, working backward is the most effective method for planning the completion of a large project. Begin by discussing with the team the end product. This may be a schedule, a set of assessment tools with teacher administration directions, a graph to depict student achievement results across the site, and so on. Once the final product is clearly identified, team members can begin to delineate the various components or steps that must happen in order for the final product to be developed. If, for example, the team is asked to create a graph to report out student achievement data for a site on a quarterly basis, then there are some obvious tasks that must be accomplished prior to the development of the graph. Some of these tasks are listed below:

- Identify achievement data to be assessed and reported
- Secure appropriate assessment tools and scoring methods to ensure consistency
- Provide staff with necessary training in administration and scoring of assessments
- Design and communicate assessment schedule
- Develop reporting form
- Tabulate data submitted
- Use tabulated data to create a schoolwide achievement graph

As you can see, this one project involves the completion of numerous critical tasks. Once teams have delineated the various tasks that need to be accomplished, they should organize them in time order and then assign intermittent deadlines for completion. Team members may take on various tasks to draft on their own and bring back to the team for review, or a team may wish to move through each of the sequenced tasks together as a larger group. Discussions related to the accomplishment of these smaller tasks drive the development of leadership team meeting agendas. This process of clearly stating the end outcome, identifying and sequencing tasks that must be completed to reach the goal, and then assigning deadlines for smaller task completion along the way will ensure that leadership teams are successful at completing projects to meet deadlines.

In addition to planning content of meetings a leader must also consider the desired manner in which the team will operate. A team's ability to collaborate and effectively communicate with one another is imperative to team success. Thus, a leader will need to ensure that collaboration and communication are fostered by embedding applicable activities in the leadership team's meeting agenda. In addition, as teams are forming, time should be dedicated to establishing group norms and reaching agreements related to guidelines and processes to be used in decision making. Although these types of activities initially take time away from content, once in place they will allow the group to move forward more efficiently later on. (See the Resources section for texts to provide activities for developing effective teams.)

The final step to ensuring the success of a leadership team is to provide individuals with a summary of meetings. Team members can rotate the responsibility of formulating a brief meeting summary of each meeting, or one individual may wish to take on this role for the group. The summary should include tasks accomplished, agreements made, and identified next steps. This running summary can be distributed to the full staff as well, in an effort to keep everyone up to date on the team's work. This summary will serve as a record of the team's work and will be a valuable reference for the group if related questions and/or issues are brought to the table at a later date.

Chapter Review

A site leadership team is a powerful tool for gaining greater commitment from all staff members. Although the development of a leadership team, in and of itself, will not guarantee full staff commitment, when carefully directed by an instructional leader it can be a productive vehicle for completing tasks in which all staff members are represented, dispersing and sharing critical information among staff, and increasing the knowledge base of everyone. In order for these important goals to be reached there are critical aspects to consider when developing and implementing a site-based leadership team.

Developing and prioritizing leadership team outcomes should be done by the entire staff. This ensures that all members are clear on the purpose of the team and the role of its members. Teams should be representative of all staff members, yet should be small enough to complete tasks efficiently.

Leadership teams do not simply develop and succeed without guidance. It is the leader's responsibility to schedule meetings, plan processes and activities for group engagement, keep the team focused on identified outcomes, and keep communication open and effective. Also, it is up to the building leader to design ways for team members to update and gain input on a regular basis from the groups whom they represent. This two-way communication between team members and the rest of the staff is foundational to successful leadership teams.

Chapter 9

Using Data to Empower and Gain Staff Commitment

"People do not argue with their own data." This is one of Bob Pike's underlying rules, and it has always held true for me as an educational leader. When data are collected and analyzed by teams or department members on a regular basis, they become a powerful vehicle not only for prompting individuals to make instructional changes, but also to take hold of the reins with a newfound sense of purpose and design their own destiny in the classroom. Of course, this widespread empowerment can lead to chaos if a leader is not prepared and equipped to serve as a guide to ensure that there is not only continuity among and between levels, but also commitment from all staff members to reaching the identified schoolwide goals.

This chapter focuses on the two hats that a leader must be able to wear in regard to using data. The first is that of the knowledgeable and experienced tour guide who not only can discern what data are important to collect but also can analyze and interpret schoolwide data to determine trends as well as professional development needs. The second hat is that of the law enforcement officer who must remind individuals of the ground rules or expectations, hold each member accountable for his or her commitments, and keep individuals focused and heading in the same direction.

Serving as the Tour Guide

There are a number of tasks that come along with the tour guide hat. First, a leader must carefully scout out the territory to familiarize him- or herself with types of data that would be useful in showing student growth toward identified goals. To ensure continuity and to be able to effectively use data to identify schoolwide trends and professional development needs, the leader must see that data related to schoolwide goals are collected across all levels and from as many disciplines as is realistic. Of course, assessment tools may vary from one grade to the next in order to meet students' abilities and developmental levels, but the general type of data should be the same. For example, if a site has identified improving students' writing ability as demonstrated through the effective use of the stages of the writing process, then each level or each department would need to collect data to demonstrate students' proficiency in each of the stages of the writing process appropriate for the students' identified level. Ensuring this consistency allows results to be analyzed and reported on a schoolwide basis and trends to be recognized. Of course, not all instructors would be able to accurately assess students' abilities on certain proficiencies. For example, at the secondary level, performing arts instructors or speech teachers may not be able to gather data related to students' proficiency in applying problem-solving strategies, but they would be able to gain information and report on students' proficiency related to oral presentation and persuasive discourse.

A second task taken on by the leader as "tour guide" is to report schoolwide data on a regular basis to staff, parents, district personnel, and community members in a clear and meaningful manner. Visual displays in the form of graphs or charts are generally most effective. These visuals should not only show current school results, but also should depict past results and the identified goal. Seeing student progress visually will motivate staff members and serve as a reminder of the fruits of their labor. Of course time lines related to data collection should be identified in advance. Refer to Chapter 3 for information related to systems and time frames for data collection.

Team Analysis and Goal Setting Meetings

In addition to creating charts or graphs to display results, leaders must also guide staff members in analyzing grade-level, department, or individual teacher data in order to make instructional decisions. This involves directing teams in identifying short-term goals to focus on for monthly team meetings. By incorporating monthly goal setting meetings data, can be brought to the table and discussed on a regular basis. During monthly meetings a facilitator, who could be the leader or a designated team liaison such as a member of the school's leadership team, can work with staff not only to review current data and set a reasonable goal for the next month of instruction, but can also guide the team in sharing personal instructional strategies used in gaining results. This collaboration focused around results can be a powerful tool in creating what Fullan (2001) terms "a schoolwide professional learning community" in which all members can continue to share their expertise and learn from one another. Of course, all short-term goals should be related to one or more of the more complex schoolwide goals that the staff have identified and agreed upon to improve student achievement. By setting up a basic agenda to be followed at each of these monthly data analysis meetings, the leader can ensure that teams use their time together wisely. A sample agenda is provided in Table 9.1.

The most effective data meetings are those that are focused and specific. It is often wise to have teams identify only one goal for each critical content area (reading, writing, and math, for example) as a focus for the month. At the secondary level the goals will be dictated by the content or discipline and may not incorporate the use of other content areas. Optimally, it would be best if each department would begin to integrate concepts and content from other disciplines in their own course instruction to provide for greater transfer of student learning. If departments are given opportunities to meet with one another on a more consistent basis to open the lines of communication and share ideas, this type of integration may become a realistic goal. Initially teams may need to begin by establishing only one common goal for data collection and analysis. Of course, teachers would need to be working on many other learning objectives and goals in their classrooms during the month, but a reasonable beginning

Table 9.1   Monthly Team Data Analysis Agenda

1. Share Results
   Outcome: Individual team members will bring data and share results related to the identified monthly team goal.

2. Review Instructional Strategies
   Outcome: Individual team members will share instructional strategies implemented throughout the month related to the identified goal.

3. Analyze Data
   Outcome: Team members will analyze team data to search for patterns and identify students' needs.

4. Set Goals
   Outcome: Team members will review long-range team outcomes and identify a new goal based on students' needs and identified learning outcomes.

5. Identify Assessment Tool and Criteria
   Outcome: Team members will identify how the new goal will be assessed and the criteria for scoring and reporting out student data for the next meeting.

expectation may be for them to bring data related to only one identified goal to a monthly data analysis meeting. Often, educators get bogged down in so much collected data that they simply do not have the time or energy to analyze it in order to effectively use it to make instructional decisions. Thus, it makes sense as individuals learn the process of data collection, analysis, and goal setting to keep it simple.

Goal Setting

Goal setting can be a complicated process. Staff members may need instruction and modeling from a leader related to how to identify and formulate a student achievement goal. Leaders may wish to introduce staff members to the SMART goal format described below. The SMART acronym has been used over the past several decades by education as well as business organizations across the nation as a tool for developing goals. Although there are a variety of terms used in conjunction with the SMART acronym, those most often seen in education are described below:

Specific: Clearly stating an objective or learning behavior

Measurable: Ensuring that the objective or behavior can in fact be monitored and measured and defining the assessment tool that will be used along with criteria for evaluation

Achievable: Identifying goals that are realistic for students to achieve within the identified time frame

Relevant: Ensuring that the goal is directly related to essential learning for students to meet identified standards

Time bound: Clearly identifying when assessment will occur and data be evaluated

Table 9.2 shows a model of a goal writing form that prompts goal writers to address each of the items mentioned previously.

Table 9.2   SMART Goals

Example: I will spend a minimum of 30 minutes within every classroom at my site during the month of January.

Goal Check √
Is it specific?

Can it be measured? How?

Is the goal realistic and achievable?

Is it results oriented? Will it make a difference for students?

Is there a clearly defined time frame for the goal?

Steps to Goal Attainment
What specific steps will you take to achieve this goal? What is your time line for these steps?

Are there any additional resources, support, or training that will increase your likelihood for success?

Evaluation: How will you know you have achieved your goal? How will you monitor your progress?

What roadblocks do you see that would inhibit your success? How will you address them?

Team Facilitators

Initially a leader may wish to serve as the facilitator for all monthly team or department meetings to set the stage and model both facilitation and data analysis. Secondary leaders working with a large staff may find it necessary to assign team facilitation roles to other support staff right from the beginning. Assistant principals, student deans, and counselors have often had some beginning training to prepare them for this type of role. Once teams are familiar with the process and expectations, the leader can easily empower a team member to take on the monthly facilitator role. Leaders who choose to empower others to facilitate team meetings will need to keep abreast of accomplishments and needs by meeting with facilitators on a monthly basis. In a monthly meeting to review results and out-comes, facilitators can also collaborate and continue to improve their own skills in working with groups, and the leader can support them in their role by assisting in problem solving and overcoming obstacles that may occur. In addition, the leader can use monthly facilitator meetings as a means for ensuring consistency among all levels or across disciplines by making facilitators aware of what is occurring within the various teams. Once again, secondary leaders may need to host two monthly facilitator meetings to accommodate the larger numbers. Of course, an assistant principal can take on the leadership role at one of the facilitator debriefing meetings each month. Finally, the data shared by facilitators can be analyzed and used to determine professional development needs for the site. Patterns and trends will emerge if a leader takes the time to look for them in the data. Facilitators will also have a keen sense of the professional develop-ment needs of team members based on the monthly team dialogues surrounding instructional strategies.

Expanding the Knowledge Base

Bringing current, research-based knowledge to the table to strengthen and support all staff members is another role that a leader plays while wearing the tour-guide hat. This demands that a leader stay abreast of current trends and research from the field through reading, attendance at conferences, and participation in peer discus-sion groups. In many cases the leader will find it necessary to empower others to gain deeper knowledge and understanding related to a specific area and then to support them as they share their learning with appropriate staff members. Sometimes deepening the knowledge base and providing appropriate and meaningful professional development means bringing in an individual from an instructional department within the district, a staff member from another site, or an outside consultant who has a strong foundation in the topic identified as an area in which staff require additional professional development. A leader simply cannot be the expert in all areas, but must equip him- or herself with a general understanding of research-based instruction and then be able to locate individuals with a stronger knowledge base to provide staff with professional development to extend and improve instructional practice within identified areas.

Serving as the Law Enforcement Officer

Guiding staff members to formulate goals, collect and analyze results, and share instructional strategies is not always enough to accomplish widespread improvement that will be sustained over time. A leader must also have the necessary skills and abilities to hold each staff member accountable for established goals and expectations and be able to effectively keep individuals focused and moving toward those desired goals. In other words, a leader must be able to wear the hat of the law. As staff members analyze data and begin to see an increase in student achievement they will be motivated to continue their quest. Seeing personal classroom results is motivating, and once staff members have experienced the power of using data and sharing one another's knowledge related to instructional practice they will naturally develop an internal sense of commitment. But in some cases leaders need to hold some feet to the fire in order to get the process started. Often leaders find that staff members are willing to make verbal commitments to identified school goals and initiatives, and yet when it comes to being accountable for those commitments they fall short. Leaders must be willing to first set the stage related to commitment by ensuring that all members understand that commitment and accountability go hand and hand. Then, a leader must have the stamina to stand behind what has been agreed upon by establishing and implementing systems to hold individuals accountable for their commitments, thus enforcing the expectations. Of course, the leader also has the pleasure of praising and encouraging staff members when commitments are kept and results are achieved.

Setting the Stage

The most important step a leader can take in setting the stage as the law enforcement officer is to make sure that goals are clearly written and can be assessed and monitored. This means using the SMART goal setting formula that was discussed earlier in this chapter. The SMART goal setting plan ensures that goals can be measured and forces teams to identify the assessment tools to be used in collecting data. Once goals are identified, the leader must work with the staff to establish reporting time lines for data collection. Time lines should be set throughout the year so growth and progress can be noted and so individuals can use data to make informed decisions regarding instruction. Once time lines for data collection are set, they need to be communicated to staff through bulletins and, of course, reminders of upcoming deadlines are always helpful and appreciated. Finally, staff members need to be clear on how data will be reported. If specific forms are to be used, these should be designed and provided to staff members well in advance of due dates. Depending on the complexity of the collection forms, a face-to-face meeting on how to efficiently and accurately complete them may be necessary. In addition to the development of individual data collection forms, a leader will also need to identify how data will be compiled and tabulated once all school data are submitted. (A further discussion related to data collection and tabulation procedures can be found in Chapter 3.)

Patrolling

An effective law enforcement officer knows the power behind regular patrol. In a school situation, the leader who patrols regularly will be able to maintain a positive environment and will also ensure that staff members are heading in the right direction. "Patrolling" in this sense simply means being visible, and it is key to wearing this hat effectively. If leaders are not around, commitments are sometimes forgotten or important questions that staff members have are left unanswered. By being accessible and visible within a site, leaders will learn about obstacles and bumps in the road as they occur, which will allow them time to work out viable solutions or alternatives. If a leadership team has been established in a building or individuals have been designated to serve as team meeting facilitators, then these staff members can assist in making sure that data collection is on track and that individuals are comfortable and prepared for collection due dates.

Sticking to Your Word

The final task related to the law enforcement hat takes both stamina and tact on the part of a leader. This task involves addressing individuals or groups when commitments are not honored. It is the final stage in holding individuals accountable. If the type of data to be collected has been established, data collection dates have been identified and communicated, and procedures for reporting have been reviewed, then staff members who are truly committed will submit their information on time. If they do not, then the leader MUST respond. If a small number of individuals fail to comply with the due dates, then a personal face-to-face meeting is in order. Always assume positive intentions first. Forms may be on their desk waiting to be turned in at an upcoming break or they may in fact have turned in their information to a team mate who has failed to follow through on submitting all the paperwork to the office. If in fact an individual has not completed the required paperwork to submit, begin by asking some basic questions, such as the following:

Is there anything that is unclear about how to complete the data collection form?

Where are you in regard to the data collection/reporting process?

What support do you need at this time so that the information can be completed as soon as possible?

Even after the information is collected and all the paperwork is submitted from those who missed the original deadline, your job as a leader is not done. You will need to put some things in place to make sure that this same scenario does not repeat each time data are due. Of course, each situation is different and only you will truly know the right action to take based on the individuals who failed to meet the deadline. In some cases a gentle reminder of how late paperwork affects your work and compromises your deadlines for compiling the data for the school and reporting out progress to parents and constituents will be enough to ensure that future data collection dates will be honored. In other situations, individuals may need a closer watch and/or someone to oversee and guide the process of data collection. A team facilitator, mentor teacher, building coach, or you as the leader, may need to take on this role. Of course, no individual should need this close monitoring and assistance forever. You may also have a staff member who deliberately chooses not to comply with deadlines. These individuals need to be reminded of the expectations and consequences if they continue to fail to meet them. A direct conversation that is clear and to the point is usually the most effective way of handling the situation. You may also choose to develop a written summary of the conversation, including potential action that may result if deadlines are not honored in the future. If developed, this type of documentation should be signed by both parties and placed in a confidential personnel file for future reference.

In some cases you may have a large number of individuals who have failed to meet established deadlines. The message that they are sending you can be interpreted in one of two ways, as identified below:

> We don't think we really have to follow through with this and are testing to see if you are really going to hold us accountable. We aren't convinced that your word is gold.

> We were unclear as to how to go about collecting the data or reporting them or were not clear on the due date.

The second scenario is easily rectified. It simply means you need to go back to review the steps necessary in setting the stage. Clear up the communication, and things should be right on track in the future.

The first scenario requires you to stand up and let them know that you do mean what you say. In other words, HOLD THEM ACCOUNTABLE. If you let them off the hook, they will continue to exhibit this behavior because they will never know when your words are really gold. One of the first times I requested staff members to bring data to a staff meeting I ran into this scenario. I decided to chart progress results on the board so we could celebrate our success as a group, but as I began to collect data I kept getting excuses as to why individuals didn't have their data to report. Initially I was angry, but luckily I took my time before responding to the group in the meeting. I held up my head, adjusted my law enforcement hat, and proceeded to remind the group of the commitments that THEY had made. I reviewed our school goals that THEY had developed along with the assessment tools that THEY had selected. Then, I reminded them of the big picture, that we were all there in an effort to do what was best for kids. Immediately individuals began to apologize. I knew they had gotten my message, but I didn't want their commitment to be based on externally imposed regulations and guidelines, so I made one simple statement that I hoped would compel them to bring the data in the future. I said, "Please don't apologize to me. If you want to apologize to someone, apologize to your students. They are the ones who are being let down here, because we are trying to use the data to make the best instructional decisions so they can reach their highest potential." I never had another issue with individuals not bringing data to the table. I learned that there truly is power in internal commitment.

Chapter Review

There is a wide range of leadership tasks associated with empowering staff through the use of data. Essentially these tasks can be categorized according to two primary hats that a leader must learn to wear. The first hat is that of the tour guide and the second is the hat of the law enforcement officer.

As the tour guide, a leader must take on the task of searching out and identifying the types of data to collect as well as the appropriate assessment tools to use for gathering the data. Of course, the staff would be involved in determining the tools that would best meet their needs, but as the tour guide the leader would provide the staff with viable options. In addition, this role of tour guide requires that a leader design and plan for the reporting of schoolwide data to staff, parents, district personnel, and the community. The leader must also take on the responsibility of guiding and training staff members in the process of data analysis as well as the development of team goals. Often this is most effectively accomplished through monthly team or grade-level meetings in which staff members bring data to share and analyze. These meetings can be run efficiently if a leader takes the time to design an agenda template that can be used each time a group meets. The template should include opportunity for members to

- Share both results and instructional strategies used,
- Review team outcomes related to schoolwide goals,
- Identify future goal(s), and
- Clarify assessment tools to be used in collecting data as well as criteria for evaluating student progress.

The leader may wish to empower individuals within teams to take on a facilitator role once teams are comfortable with the routine and outcomes of the meetings. By gathering teams together around data on a regular basis, the leader can continue to increase the knowledge base of all staff members, which will lead to schoolwide improvement in student achievement.

The second hat that a leader must wear in using data to empower staff members is that of the law enforcement officer. As the law enforcement officer, a leader must first set the stage by providing staff members with training in the development of school goals, working collaboratively with staff to identify time lines for data collection throughout the year, and defining reporting procedures. In addition to setting the stage for the use of data to guide instruction and the setting of goals, the leader as the law enforcement officer must also patrol the site on a regular basis. Patrolling simply involves being visible in the school so that questions can be answered as they arise and problems or obstacles can be addressed and resolved. A leader may wish to include facilitators or leadership team members in this role in order to ensure that all staff members have the support they need. The final role associated with the law enforcement officer is one that requires a leader to develop his or her stamina to hold individuals accountable. This involves sticking to the established time lines and not backing down when individuals fail to comply.

Closing Remarks

Effective leaders in today's world must be proficient at juggling. The metaphorical balls that they must keep in the air are many, and yet they can be classified into three general categories of skills as addressed in this text: organization, communication, and empowerment. Developing abilities within each of these three critical areas is foundational to effective leadership. With this in mind it becomes apparent that leadership requires perseverance, patience, intuition, and passion to improve the education of our youth.

Statistically speaking, our youth make up 30% of our current society, but 100% of our future. Thus, as educators we are blessed with the challenge and gift of designing the future. From this perspective it becomes apparent that education is truly the most noble of professions.

In closing I would like to share with you a piece that was given to me by one of my most passionate and dedicated teachers. She said when she came upon it she thought of me, and I was both humbled and honored. May it serve to guide you in your journey.

A Leader

I went on a search to become a leader. I searched high and low. I spoke with authority, people listened, but alas, there was one who was wiser than I and they followed him. I sought to inspire confidence but the crowd responded, "Why should we trust you?" I postured and I assumed the look of leadership with a countenance that glowed with confidence and pride. But many passed me by and never noticed my air of elegance. I ran ahead of the others, pointing the way to new heights. I demonstrated that I knew the route to greatness. And then I looked back and I was alone.

"What shall I do," I queried? "I've tried hard and used all that I know." And I sat me down and I pondered long. And then I listened to the voices around me. And I heard what the group was trying to accomplish. I rolled up my sleeves and joined in the work.

As we worked I asked, "Are we all together in what we want to do and how to get the job done?" And we thought together and we fought together and we struggled towards our goal. I found myself encouraging the fainthearted. I sought the ideas of those too shy to speak out. I taught those who had little skill. I praised those who worked hard. When our task was completed, one of the groups turned to me and said, "This would not have been done but for your leadership."

At first I said, "I didn't lead, I just worked with the rest." And then I understood, leadership is not a goal. It's a way of reaching a goal.

I lead best when I help others to go where we've decided we want to go.

I lead best when I help others to use themselves creatively.

I lead best when I forget about myself as leader and focus on my group, their needs and their goals.

To lead is to serve. To give to achieve TOGETHER.

By Kathryn Nelson

Resources

Epstein, R. (1995). *Creativity games for trainers: A handbook of group activities for jump starting workplace creativity.* Columbus, OH: McGraw-Hill Trade.

Newstrom, J., & Scannell, E. (1997). *The big book of team building games: Trust building activities, team spirit exercises and other fun things to do.* Columbus, OH: McGraw-Hill Trade.

Nilson, C. (1995). *Games that drive change.* Columbus, OH: McGraw-Hill Trade.

Parker, G., & Thiagarajan, S. (1999). *Teamwork and teamplay: Games and activities for building training teams.* San Francisco: Jossey-Bass/Pfeiffer.

Pike, R. (1998). *101 games for trainers: A collection of the best activities from Creative Training Techniques Newsletter.* Amherst, MA: Human Resource Development Press.

Scannell, E., et al. (1995). *The complete games trainers play: 287 ready-to-use training games plus the trainer's resource kit.* Columbus, OH: McGraw-Hill Trade.

Snow, H. (1997). *Indoor/outdoor team building games for trainers: Powerful activities from the world of adventure-based team building and ropes courses.* Columbus, OH: McGraw-Hill Trade.

Sugar, S. (1998). *Games that teach: Experiential activities for reinforcing training.* San Francisco: Jossey-Bass/Pfeiffer.

Sugar, S., & Takacs, G. (1999). *Games that teach teams: 21 activities to supercharge your group.* San Francisco: Jossey-Bass/Pfeiffer.

Ukens, L. (1999). *All together now: A seriously fun collection of interactive training games and activities.* San Francisco: Jossey-Bass/Pfeiffer.

West, E. (1996). *201 icebreakers: Group mixers, warm-ups, energizers and playful activities.* Columbus, OH: McGraw-Hill Trade.

References

Covey, S. R. (1989). *The seven habits of highly effective people.* New York: Simon & Schuster.

Daresh, John. (2001). *Beginning the principalship: A practical guide for new school leaders* (2nd ed.). Thousand Oaks, CA: Corwin Press.

Dunklee, Dennis R. (2000). *If you want to lead, not just manage: A primer for principals.* Thousand Oaks, CA: Corwin Press.

Fullan, Michael. (2001). *Leading in a culture of change.* San Francisco: Jossey-Bass.

Pike, Robert. (1994). *Creative training techniques handbook.* Minneapolis, MN: Lakewood Books.

Ramsey, Robert D. (1999). *Lead, follow, or get out of the way: How to be a more effective leader in today's schools.* Thousand Oaks, CA: Corwin Press.